Christmas, 1993

Merry Christmas, Stephanie.

I'm afraid you're going to find
that Mitzi and Jan short-changed Florida.

With love,
Uncle Bob?

D1361093

THE SOUTH

AMERICAN DESIGN

THE SOUTH

Text by Mitzi Gammon   Photographs by Jon Jensen
Foreword by Virginia and Lee McAlester
Design by Michael Jensen

Produced by The Miller Press, Inc.

BANTAM BOOKS · NEW YORK · TORONTO · LONDON · SYDNEY · AUCKLAND

The South

A Bantam Book

November 1991

Library of Congress Cataloging-in-Publication Data

Gammon, Mitzi.
The south/text by Mitzi Gammon; photographs by Jon Jensen;
foreword by Virginia and Lee McAlester;

p. cm.–(American Design)
Includes bibliographical references.
ISBN: 0-553-07550-0
1. Architecture, Domestic–Southern States.   2. Vernacular architecture–Southern States.
3. Interior decoration–Southern States.   I. Jensen, Jon.   II. Title.   III. Series.
NA 7211.G35   1991   728′.37′0975–dc20   91–9396   CIP

Published simultaneously in the United States and Canada

Bantam Books are published by Bantam Books, a division of Bantam Doubleday Dell
Publishing Group, Inc. Its trademark, consisting of the words "Bantam Books"
and the portrayal of a rooster, is Registered in U.S. Patent
and Trademark Office and in other countries, Marca Registrada.
Bantam Books, 666 Fifth Avenue, New York, New York 10103.

Printed in Italy by New Interlitho S.p.A.–Milan

0 9 8 7 6 5 4 3 2 1

To my smiling Madison and Gabriel, and to Ed,
whose love and patience endures all

–Mitzi Gammon

———————————————————

To Anne

–Jon Jensen

ACKNOWLEDGMENTS

■■

This book was produced to capture the South's enduring character as a region where the love of home, family, and traditions—new and old—flourishes. The rhythm of life in the South does not proceed along at a predictable pace because the region is the most geographically diverse of any in America. Yet, again and again, these same basic values influence people where they live—whether it is the flat, marsh-rimmed coastal areas or the rich, agricultural valleys of the gently sloping Blue Ridge Mountains. One of the homeowners lives in her grandfather's house in a small southern town. Some have renovated houses in major metropolitan centers, and by so doing lent their individuality to both their homes and neighborhoods. Others inhabit houses in the mountains and along the coast that define what life means most to them. However and wherever they reside, all do so with an undeniably southern style.

With heartfelt wishes I thank them all for their patience, time, cooperation, and gracious hospitality: Van and Mary Ann Allen, Joe Blount and Luis Garcia, Jack and Patty Boineau, William and Sally Cooper, Washington and Judy Falk, Frances and James Frakes, Steven Harris, David and Alethia Haynes, Gerald and Sue Henley, Dinwiddie Lampton, Robert and Sandra Richardson, Hampton and Nancy Roy, Samuel and Ruth Snapp, Skip and Gayle Tuminello, Tom and Jackie Munson, and all who wish to remain anonymous.

Finding my homeowners would have been impossible without the extensive assistance of friends, acquaintances, and professionals along the way. For pointing me in the right direction, I express great thanks to: Bill Coursey, John English, Mary Ellen Pettigrew, Susan Harte, Robert Currey, Chris Wohlwend, Lee Walburn, Emma Edmunds, Dorothy Griffith, Todd Murphy, Phyllis Farmer, Beth Downey, Sam Flowers, Marcia Kleinberg, Jennifer Weiss, Carol Newland, René Sanning, Donna Peritt, Lake Douglas, Ann Smith, Bill Cox, Susan Stevens, Susan Withers, Alyson Storch, Wayne Wood, and Jim Stevenson. I owe a huge thanks to Linda Humphrey McCallum for passing my name along. For finding me and supporting me from the project's conception to completion, I thank Angela Miller of The Miller Press, Sharon Squibb of Crown Publishers, Coleen O'Shea and Becky Cabaza of Bantam Books. I would also like to thank Jon Jensen for his beautiful photographs and his brother, Michael Jensen, for his talented graphic touch. I also extend my appreciation to Dot Hester of the Delta & Pineland Co., Sarah Davidson, Donna Burbank, Dwight Wilson with the Beaches Area Historical Society, Thomas Blount, AIA, Mitch Wilds and Peter Sandbeck of the North Carolina Preservation Office, Robert Hodges, Ann Vaughan with the Natchez Spring tour office, Dr. William Kennedy for his architectural knowledge, the Georgia Historical Society, Joel McEachin, Ron Miller of Historic Natchez, Ted Pappas, AIA, Tom Christ, AIA, Maurice Jennings, AIA, Cal Bowie, AIA, Travis Price, AIA, Walt and Riva Upright, and the Atlanta-Fulton Public Library. Most of all, I thank my parents for my southern heritage.

CONTENTS

FOREWORD

■■■■■■■■■■■■■■■■■■■■■■■■■■

Perhaps no other part of our vast nation calls to mind such contrasting images as does the American South. Williamsburg and Cape Canaveral, Nashville and New Orleans, the Great Smokies and the Florida Keys, timeless country villages and bustling modern cities—these only hint at the rich diversity of this complex region. Both history and geography have shaped these many contrasts.

The Old South states—Virginia, the Carolinas, and Georgia—began as fragile coastal colonies tenuously tied to a distant England. During more than a hundred years of colonial rule, settlement hugged the coast until independence launched the new nation on a century of westward expansion. Settlement then spread across the Appalachian barrier to the virgin lands of Tennessee, Kentucky, and Arkansas and around the southern end of the mountains into the future New South states of Alabama and Mississippi. This rush of Anglo settlement collided with long-established colonists from elsewhere in Europe—Spaniards in Florida and the French in Louisiana. Although politically absorbed by the new United States by the 1820s, vestiges of their Latin heritage persist in these regions even today as Sunbelt migrations bring new waves of prosperity to the venerable South.

Nowhere is this long and colorful saga more vividly reflected than in the South's legacy of domestic architecture—the houses built by its residents over several centuries. This is delightfully demonstrated on the pages that follow as the reader is taken on an intimate tour of fourteen carefully chosen Southern houses. These include examples from each of the eleven Southern states and illustrate a representative range of ages and styles. The oldest, coastal South Carolina's Summit Plantation, was built in 1816, and the youngest, this time on the Florida coast, is Seashore Original built in 1975. Older houses predominate—more than half were built before 1900. Stylistically, they range from simple log folk dwellings (Hallston Hollow Farm) to grand Italianate mansions (Floweree Estate). In short, dipping into these handsome photographs and informative text provides a fascinating introduction to the extraordinary cultural diversity of the American South.

Virginia and Lee McAlester

THE SOUTH

INTRODUCTION

■■■■■■■■■■■■■■■■■■■■■■■■■■■■■■■■■

Volumes have been written on the images associated with the American South. Yet the question remains: What is it? Establishing one prevailing identity for the South is impossible because the region is so many things to so many people. To some, it is an uncomplicated homeland where hospitality and home-style cooking prevail. To others, it is the area of America still marred by the Civil War. That the South possesses a singular charm that stems from its enduring rituals, myths, and traditions cannot be disputed.

Old habits do die hard in this region where Northerners are still called "Yankees" and fried food is still fashionable. But some of the common Hollywood myths attached to the South are slightly outdated. The movie classic *Gone With the Wind* provided a popular, beloved portrayal of the South that has endured for six decades of a landscape dotted with splendid Greek Revival mansions overlooking lush cotton fields and populated by seductive Scarletts, hoop-skirted Magnolias, swaggering Rhetts, and beer-loving Bubbas—all of whom speak with incredibly thick accents.

These popular myths are handy labels for the South, but the makeup of contemporary Dixieland is so much richer and more varied.

Drive southward out of upland Virginia and watch the panoramas change. The breathtakingly beautiful Blue Ridge Mountains extend through Virginia, the Carolinas, and northern Georgia. Along this drive, Tennessee's rolling, verdant farmlands become the red-clay foothills of Georgia. Farther south, pristine white-sand beaches edge the coastal areas. In the areas south of Charleston down into northern Florida, unmarked dirt roads veer off paved streets beneath centuries-old live oak trees cloaked in graceful strands of Spanish moss. Prickly silhouettes of palmetto bushes punctuate the scrubby undergrowth covering the sandy, coastal flats of Georgia, Florida, and Alabama. Elaborate causeway networks bridge Mississippi's and Louisiana's swampy bayous.

Though superinterstates now efficiently connect all of these areas, pockets of pure Southern culture flourish along the back roads. Fleets of shrimp boats, with their nets trailing behind them like ponytails, moored beside tidal marsh waterway docks are a familiar site throughout the summer in coastal communities. Elsewhere, roadside food stands provide colorful scenes all year long. The pungent aroma of citrus fruits scent balmy summer evenings across Florida where you can drive through small towns day or night and find rows of fruit stands stocked with oranges and grapefruits.

In the fall, narrow, winding mountain roads are dotted with crudely lettered signs that point the way to roadside lean-tos where farmers sell bountiful selections of homegrown canned jellies, syrups, molasses, and glass jugs filled with sweetly tart apple cider. Boiled peanuts are a year-round snack cooked in the open and sold from roadside shacks across Georgia and South Carolina. Freshly ground and grilled boudin—a type of sausage—can be enjoyed throughout lower Louisiana and Mississippi.

The voices of the South are as rich and diverse as its landscapes and cuisine. A true Southern accent is soft and melodic. Accents vary from area to area: A native Tidewater Virginian's proper English lilt bears little resemblance to the sound of a south Lousianian's Cajun French-derived accent. Ask natives to say *July* and *pecan* and you will get a uniquely different pronunciation every time. The "drawl" exists all across the region because Southerners are prone to drop letters here and there from words. Phrases such as "y'all" and "fixin' to" are still part of the Southerner's vocabulary.

The region's language is as colorful as the way it is pronounced. It is generously laced with colloquial sayings. Coke is the generic label used to refer to any type of soft drink. Southerners refer to the noon meal as dinner, and supper is the evening meal. Regional cuisine served at these meals is distinctive in taste as well as in name because Southerners are prone to give their native foods expressively descriptive labels. Hoppin'

John is a traditional New Year's dish of black-eyed peas and rice enjoyed exclusively in the deep South. Cheese straws are small snack crackers served at luncheons and teas. Though grits are recognized as a staple of Southern cooking, cornmeal's popularity is even more widespread. Mixed with a little egg and buttermilk, this ingredient is used to make two of the South's most popular dining sensations: hoe cakes and hush puppies.

The South also has its own musical sound, for, after all, this is the land that birthed the blues, jazz, and country music. New Orleans's piano-playing crooner Harry Connick, Jr., and the trumpet-blowing Wynton Marsalis as well as Georgia's godfather of soul, James Brown, and other legendary greats claim the South as their homeland. One of the region's biggest contributions to the world of popular music was the King—Elvis Presley—who grew up in Tupelo, Mississippi, and built his Graceland showpiece estate in Memphis, Tennessee, after topping the charts and establishing himself as a legend.

The Hollywood interpretations of life in the South are as diverse as the many ways the small-town charm of Mayberry differs from the folksy comfort of Walton's Mountain or the old-world glamour of Tara. Notables such as William Faulkner, Flannery O'Connor, Tennessee Williams, Truman Capote, and, more recent, Pat Conroy and Alice Walker tapped into the familiar sights and sounds of their native region to win literary fame. All penned informed narratives about their perceptions of life in the South. In doing so, they imbued the region with a special blend of real-life earthiness and quirkiness portrayed by colorful characters ranging from opinionated good ol' boys to high-strung Southern belles. Typically, their works reflect the region's emphasis on decency, forthrightness, loyalty, and love of family.

Craft traditions of the past are alive and well all across the South. In a region where at least one bed in almost every household is warmed by an heirloom quilt, the handmade item is now equally if not more valued than the mass-produced one. Craft fairs and festivals are eagerly anticipated and heavily attended annual events. This widespread support and demand for the traditional have young potters, weavers, and other craftspeople working in the centuries-old traditions of the past.

Even with this list of accomplishments, the South's reputation as a cultural center has been widely disputed. The region's standing in this area has changed enormously since H. L. Mencken proclaimed it the "Sahara of the Bozarts" a half century ago. One example of advancement is how architectural preservation has become an important social issue ingrained in the mainstream Southern consciousness. Architectural historian Mills Lane describes the region's varied mix of architectural treasures as "three-dimensional history books which reflect the comings and goings, successes and failures of real people." Residents of Charleston, South Carolina, were pioneers in architectural preservation. In 1931, they protected their gracious seaport city's stately public buildings, churches, and residences by approving the nation's first historic district ordinance.

Other communities now understand the precautions Charlestonians took as regional emphasis shifts away from a policy of demolition that once valued all-modern developments. The move toward preservation is a welcome change for a region where, until a few years ago, the wrecking ball loomed over many historic districts.

All across the region, the South is dotted with a variety of architectural styles that range from Georgian mansions to Federal town homes and Victorian cottages. Still, Greek Revival with the charm of shaded verandahs and massive columns is most frequently associated with the South. Only the aristocratic and privileged settlers were fortunate enough to set up house in such stately structures. The presence of one-story hall-and-parlor and dogtrot structures was more widespread than glamorous estate homes. As the region's inhabitants prospered, their houses became larger and more detailed.

Many early Southerners were forced to rely on materials at hand to construct their homes instead of on mass-manufactured materials. In the poorer rural areas, homes were built of rough board and batten or crude log construction according to whichever was the cheapest and most abundant. Only manor homes were built of brick because the affluent classes were the only ones who could afford the expense of masonry construction. Tabby was another popular material used exclusively among coastal-area residents. Brought to America by the Spaniards, the labor-intensive mortarlike material was mixed from sand, lime, oyster shells, and water and then

5

poured into forms and commonly used for foundations, walls, floors, and roofs. The South still benefits from the early widespread use of durable brick and tabby construction, because more of the region's historic homes survived the ravages of weather, fire, and flood.

Climate also impacted on the way early Southerners constructed their homes. One-story structures were more common than two-story houses all across the South because the region's milder winters did not necessitate additional interior spaces beyond bedrooms and a common space as it did in more northern areas. Kitchens were located outside the main houses so that the activity of cooking would not overheat living areas during humid summers. Latticed plantation shutters were favored because these window treatments kept the sun out and allowed breezes in. Following the example set by settlers in the West Indies, the early Southern English colonists modified the narrow stoops on their homes into spacious porches so that the noonday sun could not beat directly into the houses. These practical architectural elements evolved into a hallmark of Southern living.

Front-porch hospitality is one Southern tradition that survives unblemished. Even the most reserved Southerner is genuinely polite to strangers. Children are taught to say "yes, ma'am" and "yes, sir" with great frequency, and waving is a regional pastime. Natives are quite prone to wave at anyone—family, friends, casual acquaintances, strangers—from their cars, porches, yards, and boats and generally feel offended when the gesture is not warmly reciprocated.

This eagerness to meet and greet extends from the spirit of family that touches every aspect of the Southern life-style, whether it is a house that has been passed down through the family year after year, a priceless heirloom antique decorating a room, or a name passed from grandparent to parent to child. This strong family sensibility produces a regional identity that reaches beyond single households and unites all Southerners. Natives are proud of their heritage and are ready to defend their homeland against criticism.

Southerners are protective of their regional pedigree because as a group they understand in a way that other Americans cannot the threat of total destruction. The Civil War is no more than a television documentary or a historic marker to many people, but for Southerners the War Between the States looms as a symbol of frustration, defeat, and collective humiliation.

The bloody conflict rightfully ended a dark period in American history, but it also alienated the region's inhabitants from the rest of the country for many years. Union General William Sherman's unyielding scorched-earth policy in his infamous march to the sea, burning barns, destroying towns, and bending train-track rails on his way, crushed the Confederacy and brought Southerners together in a lasting bond. Attachment to one's roots is so strongly ingrained in the Southern soul that even if a native grows up and moves away from home, his or her identity is, in some fashion, tied to the South.

Though Southerners tout their heritage and cling to the familiarity of the past, they also embrace change. Today the region's essence has acquired a different tone, enriched, for better or worse, by the rhythms of outside influences. These developments are reshaping the South's traditional landscapes.

Expanding transportation routes, especially those of airlines, have affected where Southerners live. Large cities, such as Charleston, Savannah, and New Orleans, were the region's first centers of commercial and financial activities. Their eastern seaboard and Mississippi River locales made the cities safe ports for trade and travel via ocean-going vessels. The advent of the railroad dispersed the region's population farther inland and decreased the coastal cities' importance.

Today, the early centers of urban activity are completely superseded by metropolitan centers equipped with major airports. Atlanta's growing prominence on both the national and international levels is largely due to its international airport, one of the country's busiest and largest.

These larger, efficient avenues of transportation have opened the South up to a broader spectrum of people. Its comparatively low cost of living, mild climate, and emphasis on family values also makes it a wonderful place to live. More and more, businesses and individuals are relocating to the South and adopting it as their home. The wealth of traditions and rituals these new residents bring with them—whether they are from as far away as Japan or as near by as California—intensifies the region's culture.

Herein lies the real beauty of the South. The region's natural charms and homespun delights are equaled by its people's ability to gracefully absorb and integrate the old with the new. No matter how many advancements are made, the pace of life within the South remains comfortable and calming because gentle living is the rule here. Southerners continue to cherish their Sunday drives, fried chicken dinners, and biscuit breakfasts, but they are not so isolated by the past that they don't keep pace with the world around them.

VIRGINIA

Holston Hollow Farm

RUSTIC SIMPLICITY ON THE VIRGINIA/TENNESSEE BORDER

■■■■■■■■■■■■■■
A stand of hemlocks, white pines, poplars and maples shades the main house, surrounded by rustic split-rail fencing (above).

■■■■■■■■■■■■■■
Until Alethia restores it, this antique (left) corner cupboard serves as a temporary display shelf for antique farm implements and baskets.

The south fork of the Holston River winds its way out of Virginia into Tennessee, connecting a network of rugged valleys tucked away within the gentle shadows of the Appalachian Mountains. Holston Hollow is one of the river's more secluded gorges, a retreat encircled by mountains bristling with the crisp smell of white pines and the burbling sound of water racing southward against rocky riverbeds. Here, a lawyer and his wife, a passionate collector, revel in their love for horses and their intense appreciation for antique and regional crafts on a farm located just ten miles outside Bristol, Tennessee/Virginia.

Billed as "America's first frontier," the tiny

■■■■■■■■■■■■■■■
Hand split cedar roof shakes top the structures of the main house and guest cottage (left).

■■■■■■■■■■■■■■■
Set back within a frame of leafy tulip poplars, a side porch built by Alethia is a cool shelter in the heat of summer (right). Generous Malone rockers make comfortable resting spots for viewing the valley's beautiful panorama. The wood tub is carved from a tree.

■■■■■■■■■■■■■■■
The late summer blooms of a deep purple clematis vine delicately embellish the front drive's iron hitching post (above).

sliver of land high in the Appalachian uplands juts out between the westernmost reaches of Virginia and North Carolina. The surrounding land is dotted with historic landmarks such as the site of the oldest territorial capital, Rocky Mountain, and the birthplace of the mythical frontiersman Davy Crockett. Bristol is also among the area's curiosities because the state line separating Tennessee and Virginia runs directly down its center.

This town's dual identity has engendered two separate municipalities and intertwines the histories of the two states. The British were the first to lay claim to the region in 1584, through a patent given to Sir Walter Raleigh of Virginia. Settlement along the Holston River's upper waters didn't begin until 1746, when Stephen Holston arrived and undertook the task of surveying the river and adjacent lands. For the most part, the British abandoned the region to the Cherokee until the Indians signed a treaty giving away their rights to the land in 1768.

After hearing of this new land of opportunity, two Maryland gentlemen, Isaac Baker and Evan Shelby, made their way south in search of profitable ventures. Arriving in the Bristol area, they must have been impressed by the active travel route de-

Steeplechase prints reflect the owners' equestrian interests while a family heirloom "beehive" clock keeps good time. A Dresden Plate–patterned quilt is draped over an open door of the corner cupboard, which was crafted in Damascus, Virginia (left).

A vignette of wooden figures representing a "shotgun wedding" and other aspects of country living carved by local craftspeople decorates the top of a punched-tin dining room sideboard. A primitive folk art painting from the mid-1800s depicts a scenic panorama of a western valley (right).

veloping through the Holston Valley. Settlers walking and riding over Trade Gap Trail, the first opening in the mountains, journeyed directly through the valley along a well traveled route called Wilderness Road on their way through the Cumberland Gap and on out into America's heartland. Undoubtedly convinced the heavily trafficked mountainous avenue made the area an ideal location for development, the men purchased 1,946 acres from the heirs of Colonel John Buchanan.

They settled the area already called Sapling Grove in 1772 and divided the parcel in half, giving Baker the Virginia portion and Shelby the Tennessee tract. After forty years, Baker relocated his family north back into Virginia around the community of Abingdon. Shelby remained and built a trading post and fort that was frequented by early American frontiersman Daniel Boone on his trips in and out of untamed wilderness territories.

In 1856, the settlement's divergent origins split it apart during its incorporation. The Tennesseans chose the name Bristol, after the town of the same name in England. The Virginia community chose the name Goodson. By 1890, the Virginians opted to reunite the town and renamed their half Bristol. From its trading origins, the city prospered and grew into a railroad center

and shipping port for the area's rich coal and ore deposits.

Scant records were kept by the town's early founders about their routines or life-styles, but the beauty of the countryside they helped tame is still intact. David Haynes, a fifth-generation descendent of Isaac Baker, and his wife Alethia, are still in awe after twenty years on their Holston Valley mountain property, where they live with their son, daughter-in-law, two grandsons, more than twenty horses, eight dogs, and several cats. The 260-acre tract is nestled in a secluded setting bordered by the Cherokee National Forest. "We know people who have lived in the Holston Valley their whole lives who come over and say, 'Golly, I just didn't know this was back in here,'" says Alethia.

Alethia Haynes came "home" the first time she passed through the gated entrance leading into her mountain valley retreat. She and her husband saw the farm for the first time in the early 1970s when they attended a party given by a friend living in a rustic rental structure on the property. "Our friend had a picnic in the main house where we live now. The second I walked into this house I said, 'This is where I am supposed to live.' I had a feeling about it from the very first. It was the strangest feeling, but I knew that one day I would live here."

15

■■■■■■■■■■■■■■
An antique child-sized
hutch is filled with toys
for visiting grandchildren.
The cherrywood cupboard,
bought in Gate City,
Virginia, was an early
addition to the antique
collection (above).

■■■■■■■■■■■■■■
A collection of family
images—photographs,
miniature portraits, and
silhouettes—graces a parlor
wall (right). The large
oval-framed picture of a
golden-curled toddler is a
hand-colored photograph
of Alethia Haynes's father.

Family pictures, chaise
lounge, and a grouping of
cane chairs dating back to
the turn-of-the-century
create an inviting ambience
in a sun-porch nook, a
favorite family gathering
spot during the fall and
winter. The door opens
onto the open porch at the
side of the house.

A circa 1820 banquet-sized table in the main dining room extends over twelve feet. The punched-tin Jackson Press pie safe is from Scott County, Virginia (above right).

Alethia Haynes expanded her dining room area and gained a sweeping view of the valley's pond and pastures by adding a sun porch on the front of the house (below right). Entry to the new addition is marked by a carousel horse figure carved by artist Hal H. Haynes, David's brother.

Ten years later her dream came true. The Hayneses heard that the Holston Hollow Farm was going to go up for sale and bought it in 1982. Since then, the Hayneses have enhanced the valley's natural ruggedness with their collection of rustic log houses. The existing compound is proof that Alethia relishes the challenge of creating new houses from bits and pieces of old buildings. All three, including the main house, their son Bruce and daughter-in-law Anne's house, and a guest house, were assembled from fragments of houses. Detailed with mantels, floorboards, paneling, and doors the owners bought over the years, the structures resonate with the warmth and character of other lives.

The Hayneses discovered an uncanny connection between themselves and the main house after they bought the property and began tracing the structure's history. In 1968, the main house was moved from town by the former owner to its current location. Alethia's research uncovered information that indicates the house might very well be the same residence where her husband's ancestor, Isaac Baker, and his wife lived. Historical records show the pioneer couple lived in a "mansion house" in 1792 that fits the description of her own home. Even more coincidental is the fact that local historians place the Bakers' home approximately in the same location, above Bristol's Beaver

The warm glow of walnut was uncovered beneath ten coats of paint layered over a living room mantel salvaged from Bruce Haynes's house. An heirloom quilt warms the walnut bed in the children's guest room in the main house (left). The fox print is by the official colonial Williamsburg artist, John Ruthven.

Antiques, easy chairs, and a wood stove make the kitchen a cozy spot for relaxing and visiting (right). A collection of twelve locally manufactured oak and maple chairs recognized as "Malone" chairs are pulled up to a pine lazy-Susan table dating from the mid-1800s.

Creek, where the Hayneses' home originally sat.

Since the house was primarily intended as a weekend lodge, it was drafty and rough when the Hayneses first moved in. Yet they were so eager to live on the property that they did not upgrade the house before moving in. The main house is a combination of two structures—the relocated Bristol house and a log barn the previous owner had moved to the property from nearby Hickory Tree, Tennessee. The two buildings were connected by an open-air dogtrot. The Haynes found this arrangement, though adequate for weekend use, unsuitable for year-round living. The insulation was so poor the roofing shakes were visible through the kitchen ceiling. "We had to go outside to go to the kitchen," says Alethia. "My son used to laugh and say, 'You don't have to fix coffee to wake up in the morning, because walking outside in the winter is a real eye-opener.'"

After enduring two years of frost exposure, Alethia tackled the job of framing up the dogtrot enclosure herself with the aid of a do-it-yourself carpentry book. When her husband and son returned later in the evening on the first day of her project and questioned her about the workman's identity, she replied,

"You're looking at her." The addition now functions as a connecting wing between the kitchen and the rest of the house and also accommodates a dining room.

Installing creature comforts such as insulation and a wood-burning stove were the top priorities once the hallway addition was complete. A tin roof replaced the kitchen wing's original leaky roof. The owners then turned their attention to tailoring the home's living space to suit their life-style by reassigning the functions of several rooms. Two upstairs rooms were converted into one spacious master bedroom suite with bath. A downstairs room became a children's bedroom, giving young grandchildren a sleeping place in the main house when they visit the farm without their parents.

Building horse barns was Alethia's only previous construction experience prior to living on the farm. Undaunted by her limited knowledge, she learned on the job and now lists an impressive number of completed projects and even more she plans to attempt. Though she laughingly refers to herself as a "chainsaw carpenter," she readily admits the rustic quality of the buildings don't require perfection.

■■■■■■■■■■■■■■■
The rocks used to build
the mantel and hearth in
Bruce and Ann Haynes's
living room were trucked
in from Shady Valley,
Tennessee. A chair crafted
by Anne's grandfather is
covered in a flame-stitch
fabric that accents the
red leather sofa (left).

■■■■■■■■■■■■■■■
A buggy (above) seat from
Pennsylvania in Bruce and
Anne's house shares space
with an appropriate mix of
other equestrian-themed
trappings—a print of three
mares drinking from a
trough hanging over a pie
safe and a cowboy carving
perched atop the bookcase.

■■■■■■■■■■■■■■■■
A converted smoke-house
enlarged with logs
salvaged out of an old barn
dating back to the turn of
the century is used as a
two-bedroom guest house
(above).

■■■■■■■■■■■■■■■■
Sleeping arrangements in
the guest house include an
elevated cannonball bed,
named for its post finials,
with a footboard quilt
roll (left).

The heart of her son, Bruce and his wife, Anne's, home situated at the bottom of the hill from the main house, is a 1790s log cabin known as the Swatts-Dishner house. An acquaintance who knew that the Hayneses were looking for a log building called and told them about an old stagecoach stop located nearby on one of the area's oldest roads. Encroaching development had the historic building pegged for destruction when the Haynes found it. Seeing the home's unusual beaded and hand-planed wide poplar-board paneling convinced the Haynes to buy the cabin for $1,000. They paid $4,000 to move it intact thirteen miles to the farm to prevent damaging the paneling during dismantling and reconstruction.

Logs from an old building on the farm were recycled and used as materials for the building's second-story addition with balcony and master bedroom suite. Building the living room's stacked-rock chimney was a six-week project involving early

morning trips to Holston Mountain. Each morning Alethia and a North Carolina stone mason met around seven A.M. and loaded their pickup trucks with rock, which was stacked and placed during the afternoon. Oak flooring and walls in the building's original back wing were recycled as dining room wainscoting and bedroom ceilings.

A guest cabin perched on the hill above the main residence was another creative conversion. Logs gutted from inside an existing barn were used to enlarge a small smokehouse into a cozy two-bedroom home. Alethia weatherized the combination structure herself by chinking between the logs the way she had seen a workman do.

The family's devotion to log cabin living is not an accident. An outdoors life-style and collection of nineteenth century American art and antiques influenced their preference. "The sort of furniture I like and the life we live goes well with a rustic-

Several of Alethia's collection of vintage quilts, dating back to the late 1800s, are draped over a guest house bedroom's loft banister (left).

type house," observes Alethia. "We wear riding boots all day, tramp into the house, nail pictures where we want, and have Jack Russells on the sofa. It just kind of all goes together."

In the mid-1960s, Alethia began collecting locally crafted early American art and antiques. Her appreciation for what she calls "country sophistication" and "naïveté" led her to accumulate a striking array of antiques now decorating the farm's interiors. The punched-tin sideboard displayed in her dining room is her most treasured find. Friends laughed when she paid $135 for the piece in 1966. She got the last laugh less than ten years later when the Abby Aldrich Rockefeller Folk Art Center in colonial Williamsburg borrowed it for a punched-tin exhibition.

By combining pioneer architecture and regional antiques, the Haynes have filled the valley with the charm of its early history. Alethia says the farm's bygone days character is what she enjoys most about life in the hidden hollow. "I love the feeling, when you come in the gate, that you have gone back in time. You can come back in here and tell the Indians were here and you can just imagine all the other people who lived here. I hope someday my children's children will feel about it the way we do."

27

TENNESSEE

Historic Federal

A HOUSE ON AN OLD TENNESSEE MAIN STREET

When the Indians were roaming through east Tennessee tracking deer and bear, they couldn't possibly have imagined that the networks of paths they were forging through the red clay hillsides would pave the way for the advancing frontiersmen and settlers who followed the paths southward across the Appalachian Mountains and into the undulating valleys. Once through the mountain passes, the pioneers pushed the Indians out and founded the first white settlements—Holston, Nolichuckey, and Watauga—west of the Allegheny Mountains.

In 1772, the settlers established the Watauga Association, which was the first independent self-governing body in the United States, under

31

the leadership of John Sevier and James Robertson. With the outbreak of the Revolutionary War, the men's efforts to secure recognition for the territory as an independent royal colony lost momentum. In 1776, the Watauga Association was annexed to North Carolina. Shortly afterward, the association's name was changed to Washington District, making it the first political subdivision in the United States named after George Washington.

Controversy quickly arose between the settlers over whether Watauga or Nolichuckey would serve as the newly established district's county seat. Since no one felt a fair decision could be made between the two settlements, they elected in 1779 to establish a new community between the two. The name Jonesboro was selected for Tennessee's first established town to honor Willie Jones of Halifax, North Carolina, an influential and wealthy gentleman who supported the settlers' desire for recognition.

From the outset, town fathers sought to give Jonesboro an urbane presence. Lots of one acre each, laid out in a grid pattern around the courthouse and commons, were sold for seventy-five dollars each in a lottery. The town planners ensured the city's visual continuity by establishing zoning laws and building restrictions that banned the presence of makeshift cabins.

In 1784, North Carolina declared its intention to cede its land west of the mountains to the federal government. Since Congress did not immediately accept, North Carolina rescinded its declaration and left the Washington County settlers with no governing body. The settlers quickly took charge and established Jonesboro as their capital.

During the late 1700s, Jonesboro gained recognition as a regional transportation center. The same trails that had brought

■■■■■■■■■■■■■■
The Federal house, built in 1840, fronts Jonesboro's bustling main street and stands as the historic business district's only private residence (left).

■■■■■■■■■■■■■■
The homeowners converted the old shed in the backyard into a woodworking shop for Gerald Henley (right).

33

■■■■■■■■■■■■■■
A local auction house find,
the green velvet sofa is the
focal point of the parlor's
furnishings (left), which
include a Kentucky-crafted
corner cabinet, a walnut
swirl-leg table, and a press-
bottom rocker. The owners
found large portions of the
home's existing hardwood
floors unstained where
rugs had once lain and
refinished the bare and
previously stained spots to
match in a process of
sanding and staining.

the early pioneers developed into the Great Stage Road connecting all points north and east to points south and west. Stagecoaches rolled directly down Jonesboro's main street, leaving travelers off at the bustling community's various inns.

Stagecoach travel through the town peaked during the 1830s. This form of transportation was superseded just a decade later when the railroads arrived, bringing with them a period of rapid growth. The completion of rail construction in 1858 gave Jonesboro access to all major cities in the North and East.

Today, Jonesboro stands as a well-preserved living museum of nineteenth century southern Appalachian architecture. The city's historic district was the first in Tennessee to be placed on the National Register of Historic Places. Jonesboro draws hundreds of visitors each year.

During the 1980s, Sue Henley blazed her own trail along Jonesboro's main street as she walked into the Cherry Tree Craft Shop that she and her husband, Gerald, own. The couple opened the shop in 1975, but were still living in a modern house in the Sulphur Springs suburb a few miles outside the city. Their

■ ■ ■ ■ ■ ■ ■ ■ ■ ■ ■ ■ ■ ■ ■
A parlor library table is adorned with colored glasses etched with delicate enameled details collected by Martha Baxter. The platter is a Henley family heirloom (above).

35

A stained-glass window designed by Peter and Bonnie Destepheno artfully camouflages the bathroom window (left). The oak china cupboard contains pieces of Sue Henley's brown-and-white English stoneware collection. The oldest piece dates back to 1871.

Above a collection of heirloom sterling, spoons from the Baxter household hang framed as mementos alongside a small selection of Sue Henley's china butter-pat collection (right).

The alcove between the kitchen and dining room is decorated with an abstract wire sculpture by celebrated Florida artist Albert Wilson (far right).

store is located one block south of the historic business district's only private residence, the Naff Shop and House, where the couple now lives. Sue had been particularly drawn to the handsome Greek Revival residence for years.

Built in 1840 by Jacob Naff, the two-story structure served as his residence, and the full basement functioned as his tailoring shop. The Naffs sold the house in 1863. It changed hands one more time before John Fain bought the property in 1869. According to letters recently found in the attic by the Henleys, Fain began renting the house in 1895 to E. J. Baxter and his wife, Eleanor, for $12 a year—$1 a month. The couple eventually bought the property in 1929 and lived there with their two daughters, Eleanor and Martha.

Martha was still living in the house when Sue Henley became interested in it. Having never married, Martha grew up and

spent most of her life in the Main Street home. In 1986, aware Martha was getting on in years, Sue stopped the elderly woman on the street and expressed her interest in the house. A year passed before Martha invited the Henleys over.

"She stopped me one spring afternoon and said her crepe myrtle was in bloom in the backyard," says Sue Henley. "She told me the house was a hundred years old and since she knew I was interested in it, thought I might like to come over and see it. We came down that very evening and she showed me through the house and we saw the garden. We told her we would be interested in buying the house and that night we agreed on a price."

Sue now calls the house she admired from afar for over a decade "home." "I have always loved old houses," she says. "It was always a fantasy of mine to live in one. When I was a little

girl I used to call them granny houses. Owning this one is a dream come true."

The dream revealed its more complicated side when the Henleys moved in six months later. They originally planned to live in their Sulphur Springs house while remodeling the town residence. But a quick sale of the contemporary home forced them to camp out for the first five months in the Jonesboro house while they worked on it.

The couple found the house to be structurally sound, but in desperate need of what they term a "cosmetic" overhaul. Neither of the Henleys had hammered a nail prior to moving into the Jonesboro house, but they both soon found themselves hanging wallpaper and scraping paint.

Gerald worked seven days a week for two years on the house with the help of two assistants while Sue ran their business dur-

ing the day before returning home to her own renovation chores. "I would come home and scrape wallpaper until I could not stand it any longer," she recounts. "Then I would go to the backyard and dig and uncover brick paths grown over with grass. Sometimes I would think, 'My God, am I never going to finish?'"

Reshingling the roof and properly wiring the house were early concerns. When the house was initially fitted for electricity, exposed wires were simply run down the side of the exterior through a conduit and left in this condition over the ensuing years. Since the walls are three bricks thick, the owners had to painstakingly groove back into the masonry to properly install the wiring.

Smashing through enclosed fireplace openings was another major task. Sometime around the turn of the century, the house's heating source was converted from wood burning to

coal. Past owners adapted the existing system by installing a furnace in the basement, covering up the fireplaces, and running the ducts up through the flues. The Henleys spent weeks reclaiming each fireplace, all the while fighting plaster and soot.

The house's color scheme is a reflection of past and present influences. The Henleys relied on town historian Dr. Bill Kennedy's expertise to restore the exterior. Using sample paint scrapings taken from the house, he conducted a series of color studies to determine the home's original finishes.

From these studies he discovered that the front and back porches were added to the house in the late 1890s. The initial absence of a front porch was common, since Jonesboro buildings were constructed flush with the property line, with no porch or stoop. Residents simply stepped directly from the sidewalk into the structures. The front porch's design is also more true to the home's Greek Revival style, while the back porch, though built at the same time, is purely utilitarian in design. The relative spaciousness of the back structure's covered areas and the fact that the property's only cistern is located nearby indicate that the family gathered and worked on this porch.

Kennedy's analysis also showed that, typical of the late Victorian period, the former owners repainted the front porch white the first two times. During the third painting, the porch

■■■■■■■■■■■■■■■
A punched-tin poplar pie safe with a narrow top drawer from the mid-1800s was bought with the house. Beside it stands a jelly cabinet. The homeowners smashed through layers of plaster to uncover the fireplace brickwork (left).

■■■■■■■■■■■■■■■
Rocking chairs pulled up along the edge of the back porch overlook century-old borders of ferns, begonias, and anemones, which color the spring yard with their ageless foliage and blossoms (right).

The hand-carved Victorian bedroom suite has been in the house for the past ninety years and now furnishes the present owners' master bedroom (above).

Victorian christening gowns, children's dresses, and a bridesmaid dress stored in the house from the early 1900s now decorate the attic stairwell (left).

was painted brown, a trim color associated with the period's resurgent interest in colonial architectural styles. When the popularity of this trend waned, all of the porch's columns and railings were again stained white. Today, except that the intensity of green used on the shutters is slightly lightened, the exterior matches the home's original state.

Dark and dated was the condition in which the Henleys found the interiors. "Battleship gray" is the description Sue uses for the kitchen's former decor. "The house was all dark and gloomy," she recalls. "I think the 1950s was the last time the interiors were decorated."

Before they could begin lightening and brightening the rooms, the Henleys were faced with the monumental task of stripping away four and sometimes five layers of wallpaper in each room. The interior's ten-foot ceilings complicated the job and the din-

ing room's last stubborn layer of old paper ripped plaster off the wall. Eventually the task was completed and, because she wanted "to create a sedate, homey atmosphere," Sue choose small floral prints in pastel colors over the bold drama of authentic Victorian patterns.

Martha Baxter eased the hardship of the renovation process by regaling the couple with accounts of the home's history. She was a vast resource of stories and advice. "Miss Martha had such a love for this house," says Sue. "She gave us valuable advice, and any question we would have, she could answer. She was the one who told us the fireplace in the kitchen smoked."

Yet, with all the changes, the Baxters' presence still lingers about the house. Most of the antiques furnishing the rooms were bought with the house, since the Henleys sold their Sulphur Springs home furnished. Baxter relatives gave a wal-

■■■■■■■■■■■■■■■■
An English ironstone pitcher adorns the master bedroom's marble-top washstand with towel rack. The rocking chair dates back to 1860 (left).

■■■■■■■■■■■■■■■■
Vintage containers and jewelry are clustered across the master bedroom mantel (above right).

■■■■■■■■■■■■■■■■
Hatpins and faux jewels from Martha Baxter's collection evoke ladylike elegance of the past (below right).

nut chest, originally owned by Martha's grandmother, to the Henleys.

A stash of scrapbooks and boxes stored in the attic revealed fascinating information about the former owners' personal lives. "It was absolutely amazing," Sue recounts. "Miss Martha was the type of lady who never threw anything away. There are still scrapbooks in the house with lists of wedding gifts." The Henleys donated a collection of Victorian clothes to the Jonesboro History Museum along with other family mementos. Above the living room mantels hang framed photographs of the Baxters, two of their daughters' baby dresses, and a telegram announcing Martha's birth.

With hard work and determination, the Henleys thoroughly renovated their home and in the process altered their own lives. Not only is their daily commute shorter—no more than a quick stroll down the street—but now they are active participants in the historic district's cohesive community. Sixty neighbors greeted their arrival one evening during the first week with the old-fashioned custom of banging noisily on pots and pans. The house is the center of activity when some of the neighborhood's two hundred residents gather on porches and yard and make decorations for the town's fall season. Weekend rituals include potluck dinners, and progressive dinners are a holiday tradition following the end of the annual home tour. Reminiscing about the new friendships the move has given them, Sue says, "this house has truly enhanced our lives."

Rocky Hill House

VICTORIAN SPLENDOR IN JONESBORO, TENNESSEE

I n an age of sleek contemporary conveniences, Samuel and Ruth Ann Snapp cling to the beauty of the past. Both like to say they were born years too late. They have a love affair with the ornate detailing of Victorian furniture, and they furnished the living room of their suburban home with red velvet-upholstered chairs, a settee from the 1800s, and a square grand piano made in 1873. But though the Snapps possessed many of the trappings of a nineteenth century life-style, they did not have an authentic Victorian house.

To live in Jonesboro was Samuel Snapp's childhood dream since the 1950s, when he caught his first glimpse of the picture-book city while visit-

■ ■ ■ ■ ■ ■ ■ ■ ■ ■ ■ ■ ■ ■ ■ ■

The Victorian house is located on a knoll overlooking downtown Jonesboro's historic main street (above). The owners repainted the house in its original colors and maintained the fish-scale shingles on the eves and gables.

■ ■ ■ ■ ■ ■ ■ ■ ■ ■ ■ ■ ■ ■ ■ ■

A sea of pink begonias— just some of the garden's 1,250 blooming plant varieties—border the beautifully quaint back porch, where the owners enjoy morning coffee around a small bistro table (left).

45

■ ■ ■ ■ ■ ■ ■ ■ ■ ■ ■ ■ ■ ■ ■
The carriage house in the backyard is the oldest existing one of its kind in Washington County and one room was used as the home's maid quarters (above). The carriage house is original to the house. It now serves as a work shop and storage for Sam's '38 Chevrolet.

■ ■ ■ ■ ■ ■ ■ ■ ■ ■ ■ ■ ■ ■ ■
Pointed arrows and diamonds detail the front porch's ornate Victorian design (right). The porch is supported by hand-turned posts and floored with tongue-and-groove pine.

■ ■ ■ ■ ■ ■ ■ ■ ■ ■ ■ ■ ■ ■
The owners designed the new gazebo to complement the older structures by copying trim details off porches and using the same color scheme (above).

46

ing relatives there. He was born in his grandparents' late nineteenth century home and grew up just thirty miles from the historic town in the small community of McPheeters Bend.

"One thing that always stuck in my mind about Jonesboro is that it has always looked like a town that just stopped. The buildings are all basically the same. They all look as if they were frozen in time around 1855." The list of Jonesboro houses the Snapps would willingly call home was limited to four houses,

one of which was a Victorian structure perched on the city's Rocky Hill overlooking the downtown business district. Neither had ever been inside the house, but they were both impressed by its exterior. "The house looks like something you would always dream about living in. You know, the ideal house on the hill."

The Snapps made their dream come true in 1986 when the couple living in the house decided to sell. A quick ten days later

the Snapps held the property's deed. Ruth Ann recalls, "Sam was bubbling before we even entered the house, but I wasn't convinced until we went inside. I could see more and more potential in every room. Then, when we got to the entrance foyer, I could in my mind envision what we would make it look like. After that I was saying, 'I've got to have this house.'"

The property that the house sits on has its own rich history. The first building constructed there, in the late 1700's, was the silversmith shop of William and Matthew Atkinson, the designers and engravers of the original Tennessee state seal. The property didn't become a residential site until 1878, when Judge A. S. Deaderick built a house on the lot. The Deadericks reportedly moved out of the house in 1898, after their five-year-old son Edmond died in an accident.

In 1892, Mr. and Mrs. Silas Cooper bought the house for $1,600 and remodeled it into a two-story structure. They lived there for forty-eight years until, at their death, the house was left to Tusculum College, one of the state's oldest schools. The house sat empty for one year until J. T. Whitlock bought it in 1948, and he deeded it over to his daughter Dorothy and her husband John Wood in 1956.

Wanting to see how the previous owners maintained the building and grounds, the Snapps searched unsuccessfully for old photographs or records for information about the home's past. They were unable to find any records earlier than the 1950s and believe information was destroyed.

Nevertheless the Snapps began renovation work. The exterior did not require any major structural repair, but the couple did repaint the house in its original colors. Dr. William Kennedy, the chairman of the Jonesboro historic zoning commission, collected over eighty-six paint scrapings from porch posts, trim, floors, and ceilings and the main structure before the home's original finish was determined. The Snapps learned that the body of the house was painted eighteen times and the porches twenty-two.

While the outside of the house reflected the beauty of the nineteenth century, the inside had not progressed beyond the look or convenience of the 1950s. The Snapps estimate they renovated over eighty percent of the interior. The kitchen ceiling that had been dropped from its original twelve-foot height to a claustrophobic eight feet was taken back up to ten feet. Three months were spent rewiring the house so that rooms originally fitted with only one electrical outlet would have the convenience of four or more.

Upstairs, three bedrooms open off the second-floor landing.

■■■■■■■■■■■■
The magnificent square grand piano is situated between the parlor's bay windows. It was originally bought by a Jonesboro merchant for his daughter in 1873 from New York City's Raven and Company and was shipped to the town by train and wagon. Etchings on the inside of the cabinet indicate that prior to the Snapps' ownership, the instrument had been last tuned in 1925 (left).

■■■■■■■■■■■■
Reproduction period wallpaper hangs in the front entrance and up the stairway (above).

■■■■■■■■■■■■■■■■
A leaded windowpane
original to the house faces
into the parlor (above).

■■■■■■■■■■■■■■■■
The twenty-four-foot-long
parlor is furnished with a
matched five-piece Victorian
red velvet furniture set
that dates back to 1885.
Original hardwood floors
throughout the house are
tongue-and-groove pine.
This room, like all of the
others, is trimmed in oak
(right).

The parlor's pedal-operated oak pump organ is an authentic Jonesboro piece built in 1871 (above).

Snapp's Depression glass collection, popularly recognized as Pink Sharon or Cabbage Rose, is displayed in the dining room (left).

ladies. Because bathrooms were also a rarity until the turn of the century, the Snapps' only bathroom was converted from an attic space above the kitchen during the mid-1920s. An old-fashioned bathtub was originally installed in the narrow room against a sloping wall, making it impossible for bathers to stand and dry off, and an unused brick chimney occupied extra space. The Snapps eliminated the room's problems by removing the chimney and moving the tub.

Interiors appear much the same as when the original owners lived in the house. Walls are either painted the jewel-tone colors popular during the Victorian era or are covered in reproduction papers. The furnishings are authentic period pieces the owners have been collecting since the late 1970s. Though the Snapps wanted to decorate the house in a style true to the period, they casually interpreted the ornate design style of Victorian decors.

"Normally there would have been a hall tree for hanging hats and coats in the foyer, and we have that," explains Sam Snapp. "There would have been a settee in the entrance for people to sit on, and we have that. In the parlor there would have been a big, square grand piano in the bay window, and we have that. Generally speaking, things are in the rooms where they would have been, but our Victorian taste is less cluttered and more elegant than the way people in that day lived."

The Snapps accumulated a great number of outstanding antiques before prices on Victorian pieces began skyrocketing. They continue to scour markets and auctions for pieces, rigidly adhering to their rule of buying items which are at least a hundred years old. The exception is a collection of depression glass they began in 1982 and that has grown to include two hundred items. They need only one set of eight glasses, a jam dish, and a cheese dish to complete the collection.

The beauty of the house extends to the outside. The Snapps' "pride and joy" are the perennial and vegetable gardens and the lawn blanketing the hillside. A carriage house original to the property and positioned just a short distance from the back porch balances the dramatic hillside setting. In 1990 the Snapps built a gazebo, detailed with design work similar to the arrow-and-diamond trim on the main porches, as the setting for their son's July wedding. The gazebo is ringed with native mountain fern, a popular Victorian-era plant.

The garden is divided into eight beds measuring eight-by-eight feet. The plot ran the full width of the lot when the Snapps first moved in, but each year they have reduced the size of the backyard planting bed. They eventually settled on raised

The only renovated space is the master bedroom, which is furnished with a collection of authentic oak Victorian antiques that includes a matching dresser, washstand, and bed. One of the two other rooms is undergoing renovation, and the Snapps plan to furnish the space with an antique walnut Victorian bedroom suite.

The home's facilities fall short of the modern built-in conveniences found in new homes, so the Snapps have improvised. Large chests and armoires make up for the fact that the house was built with only three closets. Victorian-era families didn't require closets, since their wardrobes were limited to three suits and a pair of work clothes for the men and a few dresses for the

The dining room table is set with an Italian *capo di monte* soup tureen, Cambridge Glass Company candlesticks from the 1920s, and Ruth Ann Snapp's prized collection of American Fostoria crystal (right). Danny, Sam Snapp's brother, created the floral centerpiece arrangements.

A ceramic mocha service hand-painted by Jonesboro resident Anna B. Shanks ornaments a dining room sideboard, circa 1885 (left).

beds as a way to minimize gardening work, and have found the smaller plots yield as much foliage and produce as much as the larger, more unruly spaces. Sam explains that "by taking better care of a smaller amount of plants, you can get those plants to produce much more."

Sam has, in his words, experimented with "just about anything that blooms" to create the garden, which brims with colorful flowers, vegetables, and herbs. All summer long the Snapps dine on fresh carrots, celery, tomatoes, bell peppers, and squash seasoned with chives, basil, and English thyme. He incorporated annuals, perennials, and wild flowers dug up and transplanted from Virginia mountain areas. The couple planted over

1,250 varieties of plants, including old-fashioned peonies, marigolds, petunias, geraniums, and begonias during the spring prior to their son's wedding to coordinate the garden with the bridal party's colors.

Gradually the Snapps have added enough of a variety of plants to ensure that the garden is in full bloom from early spring until the winter's first freeze. The couple introduced formality into the yard's country scheme by trimming juniper shrubs lining the front walk in tailored bonsai tree shapes.

Indoor evergreen garlands and boughs supplement the outdoor's fresh greenery during the holidays. Decorating for the holidays begins the day after Thanksgiving, when the Snapps

transport four pickup truckloads of greens cut in the woods. The celebration of the Christmas season commences with participation in the town's tour of homes, during which time the house is opened up to visitors touring Jonesboro's historic residences. The Snapps also host informal Christmas parties for their co-workers and entertain family and friends at formal, sit-down dinners. Each December more than six hundred people party in the house.

Living in Jonesboro has exceeded the couple's expectations and has enriched their lives on many levels. They cherish the town's strong sense of community and thrive on the close friendships they have formed over the years. "After thirteen years, we still didn't know anybody where we lived before, but here it is nothing for eight or twelve friends to come by in the late afternoon, sit down, and talk for a few hours," Sam explains. The owners never cease to be charmed by their home. They have gained a loving respect for old homes and buildings and are vocal preservation advocates. "When you consider that in this modern age there are so many buildings like this pushed down to make way for apartment buildings and commercial structures," Sam muses, "there is nothing more beautiful than to see an old home like this maintained the way it was when it was built."

■■■■■■■■■■■■■■

The master bedroom is furnished with oak Victorian antiques (left). The dresser, washstand, and bed, crafted during the late 1880s, all are decorated at the top with a carved fan shell detail. The black background floral-patterned bedspread is reminiscent of what would have been used in Victorian days.

■■■■■■■■■■■■■■

The three-piece mirror was built in Ohio during the 1880s and was previously used in a local men's and women's clothing store fitting room (right).

KENTUCKY

Brownsboro Farm

AN EQUESTRIAN'S KENTUCKY BLUEGRASS ESTATE

Kentucky's bluegrass region is legendary horse country. The area's groundwater springs from limestone reservoirs that produce the purest type of water. This water supply feeds into the state's famous bluegrass fields, which in turn nourish Kentucky's fine horses. The sleek Thoroughbreds grazing across the countryside's lush pasturelands represent the essence of the area's noble equestrian traditions.

Dinwiddie Lampton III is a native Kentuckian with a horse sport heritage spanning several generations. His family annually organizes three of the South's premier steeplechase races—the spring Hard Scuffle Steeplechase in Louisville, Nashville's Iroquois Steeplechase in May and

■■■■■■■■■■■■■■
Five Thoroughbreds watch
from their stalls (above).

■■■■■■■■■■■■■■
A tack room in the barn
overflows with Lampton's
equestrian gear (left).

Georgia's autumn Callaway Gardens race. Lampton is himself a horse owner who has competitively ridden steeplechase. He also is an avid polo player. It was only natural that horses would influence where he lives.

"I was primarily looking for a large enough piece of ground to have a polo field, which requires twelve level acres," explains Lampton. "My job was more difficult because it is easier to find that in central Kentucky than in the Ohio River area." His search brought him to Brownsboro Farm, just twenty-five miles

outside Louisville, where he now lives in a "piece of history."

The owner's cozy, two-story brick cottage sits at the end of a lane bordered by endless lengths of tidy brown-rail fencing and two large polo fields. The house is a frontier original, dating back to 1827, when it was built by James Clore.

Clore migrated to the area during the early nineteenth century with a group of Lutheran refugees. Following a trail his five older brothers blazed earlier, he traveled six hundred miles deep into the heart of Indian country before arriving in Oldham

County, Kentucky, around 1819. All his brothers had settled there in a small town named Brownsboro, so called for the early pioneer named Brown who established the settlement. The Clores reportedly bought the patent to their lands sight unseen with a bag of silver dollars while they were en route.

The younger Clore, then age twenty-five, settled a tract of land adjacent to his brothers' and built a temporary log cabin. Using the skills he refined in Virginia, he became a cabinet-maker and gunsmith. Eight years later he built his farm's brick house with the help of slaves. An entry out of his wife, Sarah's, diary dated February 28, 1858, describes the couple's life in the home: "This day finds me with my husband and servant girl snugly ensconced in a humble little cottage. But where will you find a palace that contains more love, more real happiness than in this little abode. No rich display of art is found within, and

the low windows are not darkened with gorgeous drapes...No velvet covering hides the rough hewn floor...Gentleness and simplicity, that makes the purest bliss."

As he prospered, Clore slowly acquired additional lands adjacent to his property until his holdings totaled 365 acres.

Nicknamed the "Old Homestead," the house that sheltered Clore's twelve children remained in the family upon his death. One of his sons lived on the property and passed it along to other relatives until it was sold in 1968. In 1979 Lampton bought 150 acres of the original Clore land with remaining buildings from a descedent's estate. Though happy with the property's geography, Lampton was less than pleased with the farmhouse. After standing vacant for a while, the structure had been used for hay storage and the roof was on the verge of collapse. "The first thing I said was, this house probably needs to

be bulldozed," he recalls. "I didn't know it was a brick house because it was covered with old insulation board nailed onto the brick. It looked like a mess to me because I couldn't tell what was under the insulation and the floors were covered with linoleum."

After paying for the expensive acreage, Lampton did not want to spend a lot of money on a lavish home. So he decided to demolish the older house and replace it with a modest contemporary structure. He scrapped demolition plans a few weeks later after digging through layers of unattractive materials to reveal the house's finer qualities such as its hardwood floors, handmade brick walls, and original windows.

The home now stands very much as it did in the past. Not much of a fanatic for historical accuracy outside a museum, Lampton likes to say he renovated rather than restored the home. "I renovated in a way that didn't interfere with the in-

tegrity of the house. All of the interior walls are intact as they once were."

Lampton tried to reclaim the house's original surfaces when he began its make-over. Bricks used in the walls that were handmade on the farm by the Clores' slaves were held together by mortar containing dust scooped out of the nearby turnpike traveled by stagecoaches and settlers on their way through Brownsboro. Bricks in the exterior walls were tuck-pointed to hide nail holes left by the removal of insulation sheathing. Eight layers of asphalt roofing were replaced with cedar shakes to match that which originally sheltered the house.

Lampton refinished the ash timbers that Clore had milled off the land and laid down for the first level's flooring. A rust-red stain initially applied to the second floor's softer poplar-wood floors was removed to reveal their natural wood grain patina. Lampton learned that the existing windows, which are origi-

66

■■■■■■■■■■■■■■■

A group of Thoroughbreds
pauses outside a barn on a
neighboring farm (above).
Once a timbered wilderness,
the area's manicured blue-
green grassy pastures are a
horse-country hallmark.

■■■■■■■■■■■■■■■

A set of brass horse-head
fireplace irons crafted
locally in Louisville stands
beside the dining room
fireplace (right).

■■■■■■■■■■■■■■
Chippendale chairs and a cherry table with fluted edges furnish the dining room (left). A collection of sterling equestrian trophies is displayed across the mantel.

■■■■■■■■■■■■■■
A botanical still-life oil painting that was originally part of the Hearst collection is now a Lampton family heirloom that hangs above the dining room's antique English cherry sideboard (right).

nal to the house, were intentionally installed in slightly canted window frames. Many settlers in the American wilderness used this design as a defensive precaution. Residents could safely stand at the side of a window and shoot rifles at attacking enemies rather than having to stand exposed directly in front of the windows.

Lampton did make some adjustments to the home's 1,800 square feet of living space. He had to add closets because early residents simply hung their few articles of clothing on pegs. Because the upstairs area was unheated, the Clores used to close it off during the winters to prevent the escape of heat generated by the first floor's brick fireplaces and the basement's wood stove. Lampton was able to open it up by adding central heating, and he finished the space by adding a bedroom and a full bath.

Lampton used creative construction to install the home's central heating system. The structure's solid masonry walls made installation impossible, so duct work was accommodated by dry

walls built a foot out from the original surfaces.

Snugly nestled in among heirloom antiques and furnishings rescued from family attics, Lampton has created an attractive and understated home. In comparing his life in the house to that of the original owners, he remarks, "I think about the harshness of one diary entry when Sarah [Clore's wife] was saying she had to get closer to her Lord to protect herself and her family from the dangers of the frontier. I realize how harsh life was when this house was being lived in a hundred and fifty years ago. Life on the frontier was fairly brutal, and now mine here is quite comfortable." Lampton's simple life-style is reflected in the interiors which are a combination of the barest necessities and heirloom niceties.

An outbuilding can be seen through the kitchen window. Built with the same bricks used in the main house's construction, the structure was erected to house the Clores' domestic servants. In 1986, Lampton converted the building into guest

quarters complete with kitchen and bath. He also reclaimed the farm's springhouse system by bringing a backhoe in and clearing out seventy years of silt that had accumulated in the freshwater reservoir. The spring now functions as the property's main water system, supplying water to a new barn with twenty-four horse stalls and an old barn built in 1915 that Lampton renovated to house his string of polo ponies.

Lampton's real focus lies beyond the front door. His favorite occupation lies in the daily routine of working with the farm's horses in their barns and pastures. He revels in the luxuries of his equestrian wonderland—among them, carefully saddle-soaped bridles and saddles neatly stored in a well-appointed tack room.

Polo matches are held at Brownsboro during the season from May to October on the farm's two recently completed fields. It took workers two years to construct and seed the fields with grass. The new playing fields will attract players seeking extra matches as they travel to Lexington, where the U.S. Polo Association Headquarters are located.

Just outside the front door stands a pair of riding boots the owner wears on daily rides across the property's well-groomed acreage. Muddied and many times worn, the boots symbolize why this horseman so values his life on one of the South's historic frontier farms.

■■■■■■■■■■■■■■
The small downstairs bedroom is decorated with a family bed the owner inherited from his grandfather (left). Throughout the house, painted equestrian scenes decorate the walls.

■■■■■■■■■■■■■■
Lampton's sterling silver polo trophy tops the bedroom's heirloom dresser (right).

NORTH

CAROLINA

Colonial Pedigree

A GEORGIAN-STYLE MANSION IN NORTH CAROLINA

■■■■■■■■■■■■■■■
Solid and handsome, the Georgian-style house evokes the look and feel of traditional southern elegance from the eighteenth century (above).

■■■■■■■■■■■■■■
With arms thrown skyward, the lead statue entitled *La Bresia* crafted by Florentine artisans stands framed in the crisp whiteness of the garden gazebo on the carpetlike grass walk (left).

Most large metropolitan areas across the South contain high-profile neighborhoods easily recognized by name, even for inhabitants of the region who have never visited them. Many share the common distinction of being older, predominantly established urban addresses of the city's affluent citizenry, gracious houses bordered by manicured lawns. In Charlotte, Eastover stands apart from the city's other residential areas.

Carefully groomed streets line the neighborhood. It is conveniently located just minutes from the hustle and bustle of a progressive downtown district proudly regarded as the banking center of the Southeast, where sky-

scrapers now loom across the horizon. This progress is in sharp contrast to the community George Washington saw two hundred years ago, which he described as a "trifling place."

His description was appropriate for the day when the city was nothing more than a small market town for vegetables, grains, and livestock. Virginia hunters and explorers looking for new opportunities first came into the territory they called "South Virginia." The population increased just prior to 1763 and the Revolutionary War, when a large group of German immigrants migrated there from Pennsylvania. In 1765 colonists named the town Charlotte in honor of King George III's wife. By 1820, Charlotte was one of only six towns in North Carolina reported to have more than one thousand residents. Later, enriched by tobacco and trade with Virginia, Charlotte's economy propelled the city to a position of financial dominance.

Cotton trade fueled the town's burgeoning economy in the 1850s and, like so many other southern cities, Charlotte began developing into a processing and trading center for regional agricultural goods. The city's pre-Civil War growth was hindered by its locale, because its Piedmont Plateau position lacked the same seaport accessibility that other colonial urban centers such as Charleston and Savannah enjoyed. This obstacle was

■■■■■■■■■■■■■■
The poplar-paneled library is the center of the home's activity (left). The room contains a carefully edited collection of art and antiques accumulated by the owners over the last twenty-eight years. An heirloom down sofa upholstered in French antique silk makes a tasteful addition to the room.

■■■■■■■■■■■■■■
Leather-bound books hand-waxed twice a year line a pair of library bookcases flanking a doorway. The collection features classic editions (right).

Thomas Holland's equestrian bronze, a collection of tortoise cases, and a tea caddy, circa 1780, by John Seymour, a premier American cabinetmaker, adorn a library side table (below).

The John Groth painting hanging above the library mantel depicts a scene at Churchill Downs. The bronze of jockeys and horses is the work of renowned French artist Fratin (right).

overcome by the surrounding region's agricultural growth and the arrival of the railroad. The city's strategic locale made it the Carolinas' major railroad center.

This development elevated Charlotte's regional profile and commercial trade. Edward Colville Griffith was no doubt drawn to the "Queen City" because it was lively and prosperous when he first arrived in 1910. While journeying from his home outside Fredericksburg, Virginia, to Atlanta, the young lawyer stopped over in Charlotte to visit with friends. He never went on to Atlanta. Instead, captivated by the promise of Charlotte's growing affluence, he remained and made the upland city his home.

Over the next several years, Griffith bought up an area of cotton farms just southeast of Charlotte's main business district. He named the acreage Eastover. In 1929, the house he built for

himself, his wife, and his five children on a hillside in the neighborhood received the House of the Year award. This first residence was sold during the Depression. In its place he built a handsome brick Georgian house – a loose copy of a Virginian manse – in 1952.

Sally Cooper, the youngest of the five Griffith offspring, and an interior decorator, was the only child still living at home when her family moved into the spacious brick house. Father and daughter spent afternoons walking the manicured grounds surrounding the residence. During these walks, Sally remembers him pointing to a large oak tree behind the house and expressing his wish that one day she would build her own home on that spot.

She granted her father's wish in 1970, when she and her hus-

band, William R. Cooper, built their own classic Georgian-style home in front of the same oak tree. Working with an architect, the couple studied houses in Yorktown, Virginia, a colonial settlement at the mouth of the York River outside Williamsburg and Jamestown that was the first permanent English settlement in America.

Their choice of architectural style was natural for a couple devoted to the eighteenth century. Georgian is the most long-lived form of American architecture since early English settlers favored the handsome style. From 1700 to 1780, an extensive number of manor houses, public buildings, and urban dwellings were constructed in the solid style. The Coopers found many existing examples from which to draw inspiration; most were made of brick, the southern colonists' preferred building mate-

■■■■■■■■■■■■■■■
French artist Louis Krakte's *Before the Hunt*, circa 1881, hangs along the stairwell beside a chinoiserie grandfather clock from England (above left).

■■■■■■■■■■■■■■
A pair of Queen Anne burled walnut side chairs and an early Georgian walnut chest make a striking entrance hall composition (above right).

An eighteenth century Adam side table with ivory pulls is a prized antique. Solid silver English pierced containers and a twentieth century Italian painting complete the dining room arrangement (left).

Oriental design adds its presence in the dining room furnishings, including a nineteenth century Chinoiserie lacquer screen and eighteenth century Chippendale chairs. The compote floral arrangement holds fresh blossoms found in the garden.

rial for their landmark plantation houses.

The Coopers' house features Georgian-style attributes: a center front pedimented gable, paneled door, decorative pilasters, toothlike dentils running along the cornice, and a row of sash windows placed directly beneath the eaves. They added wide oak-board floors pegged with walnut, and a Chinese Chippendale staircase.

The taupe-paneled library is a dramatic accomplishment. Drawing on tradition, Sally wanted the paneled library to be similar to the one in her parents' home. Because she "didn't want the red of cherry or the darkness of walnut," she wisely chose lighter toned poplar wood for the room, which receives only northern light. The richly detailed paneling, custom-crafted in Florence, South Carolina, is comprised of many rows

■■■■■■■■■■■■■■■
The guest room's decor is a
combination of French,
English, and Italian
antiques (left). A
nineteenth century Italian
painting hangs above one
of the room's two
matching commodes.

■■■■■■■■■■■■■■■
A chair and ottoman
arrangment from the guest
bedroom's eighteenth
century French duchess
chaise longue makes a cozy
retreat for napping or late
night reading. The curtain
treatment is Cowtan &
Tout fabric (right).

of intricate design elements: a dentil block, a row of egg and
dart, a Greek key, and gadrooning along the bottom.

Aspects of another notable residence influenced the Coopers'
decisions about their home and its interior. William Cooper, a
Charlotte attorney, likes to say he "grew up in the eighteenth
century," a statement he explains by recounting memories of afternoons spent freely roaming one of the nation's landmarks—
Montpelier. William can truthfully call the Orange County,
Virginia, home of President James Madison one of his frequent
childhood haunts because his aunt lived on the property as a
resident caretaker before it was acquired by the National Trust
for Historic Preservation and opened to the public.

Having such personal exposure to an historic treasure left
William with a lasting reverence for fine old collectibles and
classical architecture.

The Coopers' house is filled with the spirit of William's love
for fine antiques and for the way different periods and styles
complement one another. He spent the past twenty-eight years

■■■■■■■■■■■■■■■
This commode in the guest
bedroom is flanked by a set
of eighteenth century
French side chairs (left).

■■■■■■■■■■■■■■■
Soft elegance dominates
the master bedroom. An
eighteenth century French
settee sits at the end of the
bed. Hand-sewn Italian
silk screens flank an
oyster veneer chest, circa
1700 (right).

refining his tastes and knowledge, gradually upgrading the family's antiques as he learned and traveled. "My hobby is collecting oriental rugs, paintings, and antiques," he says. "I am a collector of art of all types and I have taught my sons to respect all art forms, whether they personally like something or not."

Sally echoes her husband's enthusiasm. Her parents accumulated art and antiques, and in 1933 her father donated a large tract of Eastover land to the city of Charlotte as the site for the Mint Museum of Art, North Carolina's first art museum. Sally started her own first collection while in elementary school.

The Coopers have filled their house with a rich mix of antiques and art. The scope of their collection includes English, French, and Italian pieces: an Adam side table fitted with ivory drawer pulls; a century-and-a-half old Sarapi rug; a Chinese Coromandel screen inlaid with mother-of-pearl and jade hung behind the library sofa; a George III game table; a chinoiserie grandfather clock.

A special emphasis is placed on Chippendale design beginning with the custom railing on the staircase just inside the front door. The couple first developed a preference for Chippendale antiques with Chinese design influences in the early years of their marriage, when they purchased two side chairs dated 1725. Though they were struggling newlyweds, they sacrificed small luxuries so they could purchase the pair of chairs. Their collection now includes eight dining room chairs, a card table, and a rare upholstered mahogany side chair.

The couple's shared enthusiasm for equestrian themes also asserts itself in the home's interior. Sally grew up with horses as her father was an original member of Charlotte's polo team. She began riding at age three and is a former Master of Foxhounds and participates annually in the Thanksgiving-to-March hunt season.

Though William does not ride horses, he is an avid connoisseur of the sport. Because his uncle was a horse trainer in Vir-

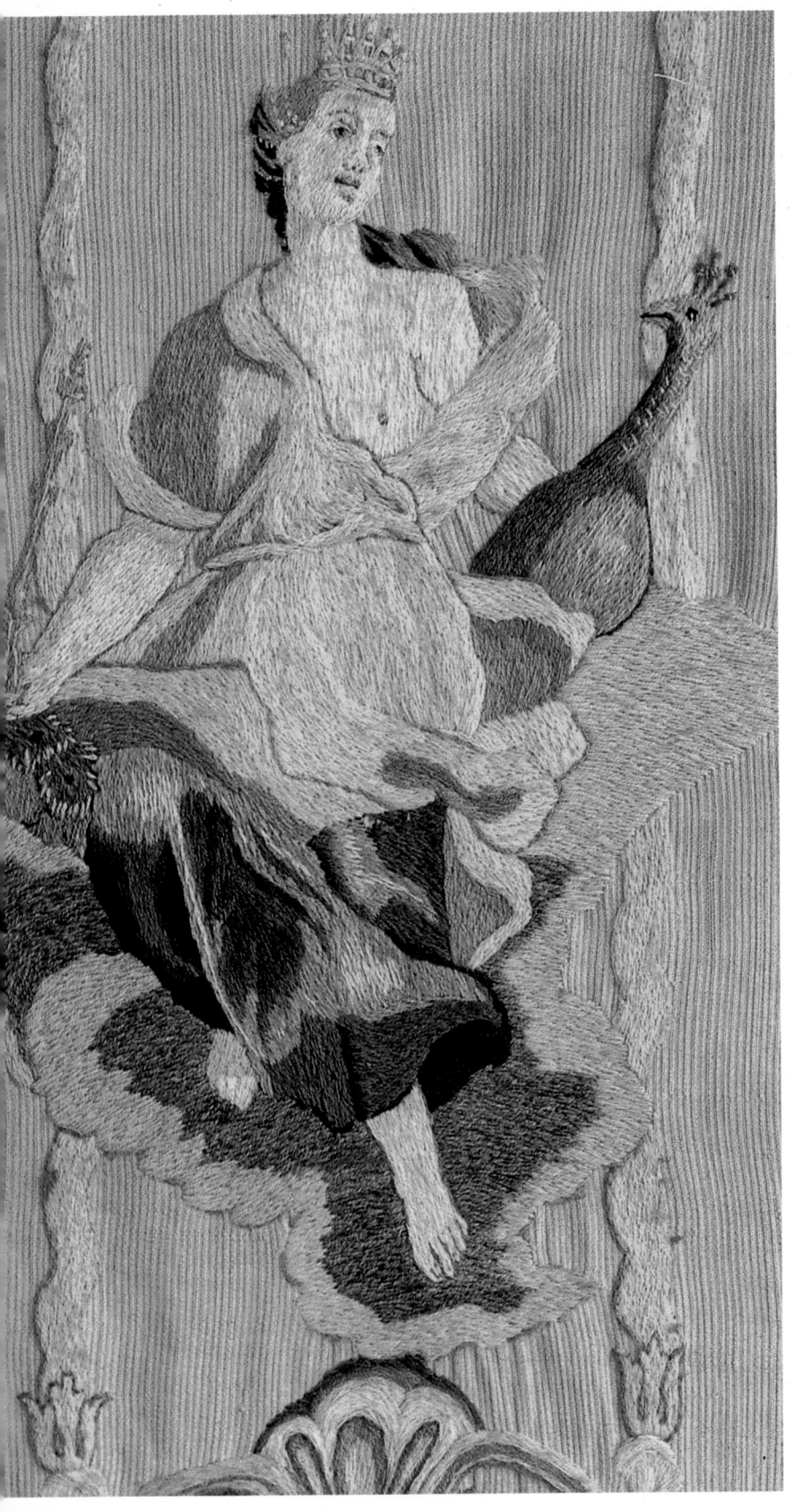

ginia, William went to shows and races as a youth. He appreciated the sport from the spectator side of the fence and pursued the pastime while attending college. "I went to the University of Virginia, which is in horse country," he says. "So on weekends, I would attend races and polo matches and follow the circuit from Virginia to Maryland. It is a way of life I appreciate."

Nowhere does the Coopers' shared hobby affect the interior of their home more than in the library. Though the room's furnishings are the finest in understated, traditional luxury, the accents are purely equestrian. Decorative touches such as framed photographs of Sally in hunting pinks, a fox hunting scene detail on the face of a grandfather clock, an antique needlepoint pillow depicting a hunt, and equestrian bronzes embellish the room.

Living space upstairs is divided into three bedrooms and an exercise and den area. The feminine pink and cream guest bedroom is filled with French antiques. A chain-stitch rug patterned with floral nosegays sets the tone for the room's decor. Fine eighteenth century chests and an Italian silk screen dominate the master bedroom.

Both Coopers can be credited with furnishing a large portion of the interiors, but the four and a half acres surrounding the house are entirely Sally's creation. The interaction of house and gardens is so important to her, she required the home's floor plan be designed so that the front door opens onto a hallway view of the manicured backyard. A board member of the North Carolina Botanical Gardens, she oversaw every detail of the plantings and singlehandedly cultivated the back portion of her parent's former estate into a lush, formal vista containing over five hundred English boxwoods. She landscaped the verdant sanctuary, which she describes as "an intimate and personal garden," so that some tree, shrub, or flower is in bloom year-round. Even the bleak months of January and February are brightened with the fragrant flowering of the *Daphne odora* evergreen and early bulbs.

In the spring the garden comes alive when over ten thousand yellow and white jonquil, daffodil, tulip, and crocus bulbs planted by the Coopers' three sons burst into bloom. Azaleas and rhododendrons present colorful pink and white blossoms. Spring, summer, and fall annuals line the grassy formal garden outside the back door. More variety is added by the blooming of Yochino cherry and Bradford pear trees, mountain laurel, crepe myrtle, and an extensive collection of daylilies, peonies, and other perennials.

Garden statuary is interspersed among shady borders and hedges throughout the garden. Some spout streams of water

and others simply lend a narrative presence to the different vignettes cultivated on the outdoor landscape. Sally enjoys quiet moments sitting on benches, chairs, and a hammock placed alongside carefully tended walking paths. She is not the only one who appreciates the beauty and solitude of the garden. Woodpeckers, rabbits, hummingbirds, cardinals, Baltimore orioles, raccoons, and foxes are all frequent visitors.

Though the garden has matured and grown grander over time, the Coopers have changed little about the home and its interiors since they first moved in. Rooms are allowed to age and mellow as the antiques grow older. Overall, the Coopers have accomplished their original goal—to live in a modern house that draws on and represents the glorious traditions and unfaltering style of the eighteenth century.

■■■■■■■■■■■■■■■

A French duchess chaise longue with a child's and adult's chair make a cozy retreat in the guest room (above left). The chaise and dressing table topped by an Italian rococo mirror are both eighteenth century. The window fabric and dust ruffle is Cowtan & Tout.

■■■■■■■■■■■■■■■

Gilded fixtures decorate the downstairs guest bath (above right).

■■■■■■■■■■■■■■■

A detail shows the intricate handwork on the master bedroom's silk screen (far left).

SOUTH
CAROLINA

Summit Plantation

A SOUTH CAROLINA COLONIAL

Du
uring the South's plantation era, cotton was the "king" of cash crops. But it was really rice that first brought great wealth to the colonial coastal regions. The golden grain prospered in the rich alluvial soils found on the outer sea islands and the banks of rivers in an area that extended as far north as North Carolina's Cape Fear and as far south as Florida's St. John's River.

A privileged land-rich plantation system that profited from cotton and rice crops was cradled in the coastal areas to the north and the south of Charleston. British planters could get rich quicker in that area than in any of the other mainland English colonies. Within the structure

■■■■■■■■■■■■■■■■■
Gateposts guarding the home's entrance are built from old English bricks salvaged by the owners over the years from dilapidated chimney works (above). The iron gate opens onto a garden setting of oaks and magnolia trees.

■■■■■■■■■■■■■■■■■
A delicate growth of light green resurrection fern outlines the majestic boughs of a centuries-old live oak (left). This backyard tree is one of four on the grounds registered with the Live Oak Society of America.

■■■■■■■■■■■■■■■
A one-lane dirt road turns off the main road and bumps along beneath a shady canopy of oak trees before ending at the Summit House entrance (left).

■■■■■■■■■■■■■■■
A covered swing is perched along the edge of the saltwater creek (right). This quiet spot, with its view of surrounding marshlands, is one of the owners' favorite afternoon retreats.

■■■■■■■■■■■■■■■
The house is supported by a tabby foundation, a mixture of oyster shells bonded together by lime, that was a popular native building material used by coastal settlers (above).

of this agrarian society, a planter's worth was equated with how much acreage he owned.

A parcel of land just thirty minutes south of Charleston along the Toogoodoo Creek possesses an extensive plantation heritage. The first man to stake his claim on the property was Landgrave Thomas Smith II who was granted ownership of a 660-acre tract in 1695. The land lay dormant until 1730, when John Bull bought the property and an additional 133 acres from Joseph Blake, Jr., son of a two-time South Carolina governor and proprietor, Joseph Blake, Sr.

Bull was the youngest son of Stephen Bull, an original Charlestonian who traveled to the coastal port with the first group of English settlers in 1670. The elder Bull owned and resided at nearby Ashley Hall plantation, located on the river of the same name. From this privileged estate, John Bull set out to make his mark and wisely planted his lands with rice. He also built a rice mill powered by the flow of the tides on the east bank of Swinton Creek, one of five tributaries trailing off the Toogoodoo Creek.

Upon John Bull's death in 1797, the property passed on to his widow, and was later sold to their grandson-in-law Pierce Butler, one of the state's first two U. S. senators and a signer of the Constitution. Eventually, the property found its way into the hands of an affluent Edisto Island cotton planter named Major Daniel Jenkins, who bought the plantation prior to 1801 at a tax sale and willed approximately five hundred acres to his daughter, Amarinthia, and her husband, William Wilkinson.

The couple temporarily resided in the original Bull house, which by then was appropriately nicknamed "Rat Hall," due to its dilapidated state. They oversaw the planting and harvesting of their Sea Island cotton and rice fields until 1816, when they were prosperous enough to begin construction of a new house.

Completed three years later, the structure was named Summit House because the house represented the "summit" of Amarinthia's happiness. The tall, Federal-style frame dwelling is dramatically positioned on a gently sloping bluff in a shady setting of majestic live oaks, pines, magnolias, and cedar trees overlooking a winding tidal creek. An unbroken expanse of salt

93

marshes stretches out in front and beside the house. The simple cypress-shingled farmhouse-style structure with a gabled roof was originally framed in front with a generous piazza that functioned as both an outdoor room and as a shelter against the hot midday sunlight.

The historic structure stood faded and dilapidated when Jack Boineau, an area native, first saw it on an early morning fishing trip along the nearby Swinton Creek in the late 1950s. Unpainted and weathered gray, the house was a neglected landmark from a bygone era. The front porch had collapsed and been replaced with a crude front stoop; the house had no screens, hot water, air-conditioning, or heat.

This state of disrepair had not improved when Jack got his first close look at the Summit property in the early 1960s. In 1966, Jack and his wife, Patty, bought the property when a Wilkinson heir approached them with the offer to sell. Jack, who is a master wood craftsman, recalls, "The more I looked at the house, the more I admired the work that originally went into it. I felt it deserved to be restored to the shape it was in when our nation was still very young."

Jack's initial attraction to the house deepened as he searched records for information on the property's history. He learned that Thomas Smith, the man to whom the original land grant

■ ■ ■ ■ ■ ■ ■ ■ ■ ■ ■ ■ ■ ■ ■
Designs popular during the Federal era, such as the sunburst motif and reeded pilasters, are carved into the front parlor's original wood fireplace mantel (left). White pine, instead of the customary cypress, was used for most of the interior woodwork and moldings.

■ ■ ■ ■ ■ ■ ■ ■ ■ ■ ■ ■ ■ ■ ■
Patty chose the living room's sea-foam green color scheme to echo the colors of the outdoors (right). The pattern painted on an antique French prism luster reflects the greens in the room.

was made, is Patty's "six times great-grandfather." He discovered the house was also linked to his own past. His boyhood home, located just six miles away in Adams Run and built in 1838, was the Wilkinson family's inland retreat, where they spent summers to escape the swarms of mosquitoes along the swampy marshlands.

After first buying the house, the Boineaus spent winters inland and summers fishing and swimming along Summit's inlet. "Camp" is the description the Boineaus use for their first summers in the plantation house. Rooms were primitively lit by light bulbs hanging from drop cords. The living room served as a temporary master bedroom, the formal dining room functioned as a combination den and guest room, their back hallway

functioned as a dining room and their three children slept in upstairs bedrooms.

Jack repaired the house over the next ten years to make it more livable. He installed hot water, added window sashes in the second-floor bedrooms, replaced original yellow pine weatherboards with cypress, and built a front porch to match the original one. He gave the front entrance a more formal appearance than it originally had by topping the door frame with dentil moldings and sunbursts typical of the Federal period. The family's summers at Summit ended in 1977 in order that extensive renovation could begin to make the house their year-round residence.

The house is designed around a two-story center and sits on

deep tabby foundations that protected the structure from major flood or hurricane damage over the years. This building material, composed of equal parts of sand, lime, oyster shell, and water, was introduced to Americans by the Spanish and was widely used in the construction of plantation buildings along coastal South Carolina and Georgia areas. The house's central structure was built with hand hewn timbers, pegged mortise-and-tenon joints, beaded weatherboard and Carpenter brand locks. The Boineaus consider these construction techniques as state of the art in the low country for the period.

Restoring Summit house was a labor of love for Jack, which he expressed down to the smallest details. His craftsmanship decorates the house's exterior from the six cypress columns he hand-turned and installed across the front porch to the dark gray shutters he built to match broken originals. The interior is filled with many of his creations: a gleaming handmade walnut table, the intricately detailed sunbursts, festoons, and reeded pilasters on the family room's fireplace mantel, and the eighteen doors he handmade to match existing ones. The beautifully refurbished home with antique-filled rooms stands as a testament to Jack's finely honed skills and dedication to accurate restoration.

He inherited this passion for woodworking—which he says he has done "ever since I could walk"—from his father, who introduced Jack at a young age to the craft in a completely stocked shop behind their Adams Run house. He remembers carving his first stick at age five. As he grew older, Jack considered making woodworking his profession, but instead practiced his art building fishing boats and repairing odd pieces of furniture. His hobby developed into a vocation once he began working weekends, nights, and vacations in the small backyard shop restoring bits and pieces of Summit.

In his restoration efforts, Jack strove to replace missing interior details with duplicates he crafted to make as authentic as possible. He camouflaged wiring for new overhead lighting in the living room with plaster medallions, and repaired living and dining room moldings with closely matched duplicates. His only major modification to the house was the conversion of a back warming room and pantry area behind the dining room into a modern tiled kitchen lined with cypress cabinets. Jack worked with materials authentic to the home's design in the kitchen just as he did throughout the house. He crafted the wall-to-wall cabinets from an aged cypress barn brought from an adjacent property.

A Sheraton table, Hepplewhite chairs, a Battenburg lace cloth, and a hand-painted Coalport fruit tazza from 1820 appoint the formal dining room (left).

A walnut sideboard inlaid with maple is an original Jack Boineau copy of the facade of a sideboard displayed in the Museum of Early Southern Decorative Arts (above).

Inherited and collected treasures fill the shelves of an English mahogany china cabinet. Air twist stem goblets displayed on the top shelf are Williamsburg reproduction designs (right).

In 1982, with the help of architect Jack Mitchell, the Boineaus added a master bedroom on one side of the house and a family room wing on the other to balance the house properly and expand their living space. Professional workmen laid the foundations and put up the studs, sheet rock, and framing before setting in window sashes made by Boineau and fitted with panes of glass salvaged from a local plantation of the same period. He recycled wood from a nearby yellow pine cotton barn so floors in the new rooms would closely match the house's original boards.

Jack Boineau milled museum-quality interior details to decorate both rooms. His molding work echoes originals dis-

played in North Carolina's Museum of Early Southern Decorative Arts. The museum showroom is built with elements salvaged from the elegant Federal-era White Hall plantation that was covered by a hydroelectric project beneath Lake Moultrie. White Hall's former owners granted Boineau permission to duplicate the Berkeley County estate's details and gave him some of the original pieces of molding and the mantel that are now installed in Summit's master bedroom.

As the Boineaus look back, they are grateful they found Summit in its original, unrestored state. Like so many Charleston-area families, the Wilkinsons suffered financial ruin at the end of the Civil War and were unable to maintain their comfortable

The master bedroom's Santo Domingo mahogany poster rice bed is a Charleston original crafted in 1790 (left). Charleston reproduction fabric was used for the canopy and dust ruffle. The fireplace mantel was taken from Whitehall plantation house, the same house from which a room now displayed in Winston Salem, North Carolina's Museum of Early Southern Decorative Arts was taken.

An American mahogany secretary restored by Jack Boineau to a cinnamon-colored luster is filled with books from the home's original library (right).

life-styles and large estates. Though Summit House was not burned during the war or destroyed by natural disaster, the Wilkinsons could not afford to update its Federal design when the architectural style went out of fashion, and left the house in its original condition.

"Summit is a case in which the old saying 'Too poor to paint and too proud to whitewash' applies," says Patty Boineau. "The fact is that poverty preserved the Charleston area. Because people around here did not have money after the Civil War, all the buildings that survived were left in a time vacuum."

The house is furnished with fine English and American antiques that Jack Boineau rebuilt and restored in addition to the pieces he made himself. Forever resourceful with materials, he crafted a tripod side table in the front parlor from a walnut tree felled during a hurricane. Jack is proudest of a restored Charleston lowboy chest that he estimates dates back to 1740. He instantly recognized the value of the piece when he found it in a local estate's kitchen, where it was being used as a chopping table. He replaced the drawers, lengthened the legs, and burnished the wood to a glossy chocolate finish. Now fully restored, the chest sits prominently among other fine antiques in the front parlor.

The Boineaus' property extends from the shrimp-filled inlet across a thirty-four-acre pastoral setting of manicured lawns,

sunken gardens, and sprawling oak trees. On many afternoons grandchildren visiting from their nearby homes freely run about the vast property, filling the air with lighthearted giggles and laughter as they play chase and hide-and-seek in and around the house.

Down by the river, the Boineaus keep two boats—a smaller one for fishing and a larger one for cruising—protected beneath a covered dock. In the spring, while the weather is cool and the insect population is low, friends and family entertain themselves with evening creekside dinners of fresh fish and shrimp that Patty catches earlier in the day.

When South Carolina summer temperatures and humidity climb to an unbearable high, the family plans social events designed to avoid the heat. They enjoy long visits on late afternoon boat rides up the tidal creek to the ocean's edge or linger over freshly brewed pitchers of iced tea beneath the cool respite of the front porch's shade.

The Boineaus can now spend weekends enjoying simple pursuits. Their five years of hard work paid off when, in 1982, Summit House was awarded the distinctive honor of a listing in the National Register of Historic Places. The couple appreciates the esteemed acknowledgment, but they actually got what they wanted long ago when they bought the house. That's the day when they became the owners and caretakers of a classic symbol of America's historical and architectural heritage—the southern plantation home.

■ ■ ■ ■ ■ ■ ■ ■ ■ ■ ■ ■ ■ ■ ■
Entry to the house is gained through the cool retreat of a wide shed-style porch (left). When restoring the porch, Jack Boineau hand-turned six tall columns from solid cypress on a lathe.

■ ■ ■ ■ ■ ■ ■ ■ ■ ■ ■ ■ ■ ■ ■
A front porch hummingbird feeder attracts the delicate birds on their spring and fall migrations through the area (right).

Appalachian Cabin

A SOUTH CAROLINA MOUNTAIN LOG HOUSE

■■■■■■■■■■■■■■■
Van's Camp was once a former square dance hall and canteen built in 1946 as part of a children's camp (above). The renovated one-story structure is now a four-bedroom mountain getaway.

■■■■■■■■■■■■■■■
An antique quilt panel hanging behind a back bedroom door mirrors the room's soft pastel colors (left).

Once labeled "the fog end of creation" by a Charleston bishop in the early nineteenth century, South Carolina's northwestern back country is now a region treasured for its regal mountainous landscapes. The scenic vistas were unknown to early Americans until the frontier Indian wars ended in the 1760s. Then, remote townships first laid out in 1730 along inland rivers began attracting a diverse group of colonists. Pennsylvania and Virginia emigrants and coastal plains settlers of modest means trying to escape the aristocratic plantation areas ventured into the region. Although reminders of these early pioneers are few, the unspoiled natural beauty of the land they set-

■■■■■■■■■■■■■■■■
A row of rocking chairs where the owners sit and enjoy a view of the river stretches across the concrete-floor front porch (left). Large wooden shutters across the front of the house are closed in the winter for warmth.

■■■■■■■■■■■■■■■■
This album-patterned quilt draped across the front railing is registered as an Appalachian heirloom with South Carolina's McKissick Museum (right).

■■■■■■■■■■■■■■■■
Mary Ann Allen's favorite gardening hat rests on a rustic wheelbarrow beneath an ivy-covered post on the cabin's front porch (far right).

tled remains unchanged these days.

Gentle mists envelop the rugged countryside each evening, rising up and loosely blanketing peach groves and softly obscuring the sculpted peaks of the Blue Ridge Mountains. The cool, quiet valleys are a sought-after summer escape for lowlanders and city dwellers. Van and Mary Ann Allen are two Greenville natives who enjoy the charms of the mountain estate they call "Van's Camp."

Nestled back among the Cherokee Foothills, the property encompasses eighty acres at the base of majestic Table Rock

Mountain. The South Saluda River runs across a shoals formation in front of the house and creates gentle waterfalls. The Allens' love of the mountain area's beauty and serenity attracted them to the property's board and batten cabin structure. They saved the house from years of neglect and gave it a new life as the center of seasonal family gatherings and celebrations.

The land where Van's Camp sits was used in the early 1900s as a site for tent camping. The property was first used by young Greenville County YMCA boys before it became a Boy Scout campground. The land then sat vacant and was rarely used ex-

cept for Boy Scout camping expeditions until Dr. Ben Geer acquired the land in the early 1920s and built a house on the property. During the summers, his sons filled the void in public swimming by opening the mountain property up to swimmers and weekend picnickers for a token fee.

Textile mill owners in the Greenville area bought the land in the early 1940s and converted the property into a summer camp named Camp Parker, after the school district, for their employees' children. The camp was run by Dr. Pete Hollis, the founder of one of the nation's first vocational-technical school

systems. The mountain property benefited from his leadership, for according to a date scratched into the concrete fireplace foundation, Van's Camp's board and batten structure was built as a square dance hall under Hollis's direction in 1946. During the fall and spring, Hollis opened the new building up as a craft studio.

Van and Mary Ann's romance with the property began around this time. They share memories of weekends spent as teenagers driving up from Greenville to Table Rock State Park when they would detour by the rustic camp, which Van had al-

105

■■■■■■■■■■■■■■■■
In the corner of the living room sits an English bleached pine cupboard filled with blue Willow and ironstone porcelains (above). A triple Irish chain quilt from the early 1900s hangs on the wall behind a grouping of willow-twig furniture crafted by South Carolinian Danny Shelley.

■■■■■■■■■■■■■■■■
Upholstered armchairs and sofas in the cabin's main room are slipcovered in Waverly Cranston plaid and Cranston checks (right). An antique water bench that now serves as a coffee table originally functioned as a stand for water buckets outside a back door.

■■■■■■■■■■■■■■■■
The green-stained pine hunt table, circa 1850, is from North Carolina. The top is decorated with a set of antique brass and iron measuring scales and a handwoven reproduction textile in a pattern from the 1700s. The Fanny D. Allen watercolor depicts Mary Ann and Van working on the property (left).

■■■■■■■■■■■■■■■■
A table inside the front door sits beside one of the structure's untrimmed wooden main support timbers (right). The hand-crafted mirror was a housewarming present from a family friend.

■■■■■■■■■■■■■■■■
A pine table built for a North Carolina boardinghouse was previously used as a barn worktable (below). A handmade punched tin chandelier illuminates the table. The centerpiece is an early 1900s tin and copper watering can filled with an arrangement of field flowers. The candlesticks were farm utensils originally used to clean animal skins. An Appalachian berry bucket hangs in the back corner beside an antique metal and wood handsaw. An antique American flag with forty-eight stars is tucked up in the rafters.

ready determined to be "the prettiest place in the world."

The property was passed along to Furman University, just twenty minutes away, when the Greenville school districts were consolidated. A college band camp operated on the grounds part of the time and the cabins and acreage were rented out to churches and other groups for retreats the remaining time. Many of the Allens' friends have memories and photographs of summers spent swimming in the shoals. Furman enhanced the property by building a two-acre lake across the road from the river for other water recreational activities.

In the kitchen, a 1910 buttermilk-blue wooden washing machine sits at the edge of a wooden butcher-block table, which was made from a maple bowling-alley floor. The kitchen cabinets' wood is weathered lumber recycled from abandoned cabins. A handmade tin chandelier from Virginia illuminates the breakfast table (left).

Mary Ann uses old canning jars to store corn, flour, and rice. The owners maintained the kitchen's authenticity by installing kitchen countertops made of one-inch-thick solid oak timber custom-cut at a local sawmill (near right).

A collection of wire and woven baskets used to serve food at the couple's many dinners and picnics hangs over the entrance to the kitchen alcove (far right).

By the 1970s, the camp had lost its appeal and Furman put the acreage and buildings up for sale. The rustic estate remained on the market for many years. The buildings began deteriorating and the untended shoals were left open to trespassers, who filled the waterway with discarded tires, broken bottles, and rusted tin cans. It was in this neglected state that the Allens saw their childhood haunt in 1983 with a FOR SALE sign tacked up out front. They eyed the property, driving the thirty minutes from their house in town every other day to survey it and plan how they could renovate the run-down lodge into their own mountain escape.

After having many second thoughts and backing out once, they bought the property in September and began making plans to celebrate Thanksgiving in the house the following year. They didn't realize it would take two more years of extensive work before they could fulfill their dreams.

The Allens spent the spring of 1984 hauling off truckloads filled with the river's accumulated garbage. Cleaning up the water and taming the waist-high weeds kept family and friends busy through the first summer and into the fall. Thick photo albums are filled with snapshots of family and friends tackling the overgrowth and enjoying post work weekend picnic lunches and dinners on the cabin's porch. Construction finally began in September 1985 when the first stud was nailed up in the lodge in honor of Mary Ann's birthday.

From the beginning the Allens made authenticity their renovation priority. As they converted the structure into a house, they thought that demolishing the existing structure and start-

A step-back pine cupboard by the doorway to the master bedroom displays folk and antique toys (left). The wooden goose pull toy was made by craftsman David Vance.

Antique patent medicine boxes and tins originally used to package medicines fill an old shelf (above).

This handmade quilt on the master bed dates back to 1934 (right).

ing from the ground up would be easier than renovation work. But they chose not to tear it down because they didn't want to sacrifice the cabin's time-worn character—a quality they could not recreate—for convenience.

The Allens like to say they reclaimed the property and built the house by virtue of "sweat, blood, tears, and country music." They achieved their work through old-fashioned, self-taught know-how while commuting daily to the city so they could bathe, eat, and sleep in their Greenville house each evening. Building an entire house was one of Van's dreams, but his only carpentry experience, prior to the mountain project, was limited to weekend crafts and a screen porch and den he built on the back of their town residence. Using a four-inch circular saw, hand-held jigsaw, hammer, handsaw, and an electric drill, he turned the 2,300-square-foot dance hall into an airy four-

bedroom home. The only outside assistance came from the Allens' cousin, Henry Stevens, who is a professional electrician, and the occasional help of two local workmen.

The project took more time, effort, and energy than the couple planned. According to Mary Ann, "We were beginning to think it couldn't possibly be done. We would get in the car to drive back to Greenville every night after spending all day working in the mountains, and we would be so tired we couldn't even see the progress." But the Allens persevered and overcame all of their stumbling blocks. The house's comfort level was increased after installation of the indoor plumbing for the kitchen and two side-by-side bathrooms—one with an old-fashioned claw foot tub and another with a built-in shower stall.

The kitchen's design is in keeping with the look of the house's interior. Van gave the new cabinets a weathered quality by

113

A vintage wool braided area rug warms the floor of a seating area just off the kitchen. A collection of vintage store signs and game boards hangs near the doorway leading into the back bedroom. The album-patterned quilt draped across the rocking chair is an heirloom (left).

A bedside shelf holds the remnants of a blue and white Staffordshire tea set Mary Ann received as a gift from a friend, her old *Heidi* book, a metal washboard and tub, a miniature cast-iron stove, and black rag baby dolls (right). The wisteria vine settee is dollsized. A Fanny D. Allen watercolor depicts field workers grading tobacco. The iron bed's patchwork quilt is backed with a vegetable-dyed muslin; the lace-trimmed pillowcases are antiques.

recycling several of the property's weather-worn, abandoned camp cabins. He salvaged the outbuildings' exterior boards and floated the lumber across the river to the main house. He adhered to his rigorous construction standards by installing locally milled, one-inch-thick oak countertops rather than man-made surfaces. A large rectangular table original to the cabin was brought in from a covered shed and placed in the middle of the kitchen. It functions as a food preparation area and as a buffet table at mealtime.

Plank partition walls were built around the back and side walls of the great room to accommodate four roomy bedrooms. Each one opens directly off the living area and has windows overlooking the side yards. Quiet most of the week, the three spare rooms become a beehive of activity when the couple's daughter, son, and their spouses all drive up from their Greenville homes for overnight visits. Each room is a cozy retreat furnished with collections of antique toys and clothing and the luxuries of antique quilts, soft blankets, and comforters. In the summer, each room's screened windows can be opened to the brisk evening air that carries in the sound of the water splashing against the banks of the shoals just several yards away from the front door.

Mary Ann started collecting the antiques decorating the interiors after they bought the property with the help of a friend and local antiques dealer, Martha Smith. She spent weekends combing area shops for furnishings and decorative accents. She assembled an extensive collection of early American primitive antiques that includes an unusual pine cupboard painted buttermilk blue (one of the early settlers' first paints) as well as a selection of locally crafted twig furnishings. She looked for pieces that "brought back a feeling of nostalgia and good memories." The bedrooms' iron bedsteads are similar to the Victorian types she remembers seeing in the bed-and-breakfast mountain houses she visited on weekends with her parents as a child.

Folk art items and collectibles displayed throughout the house are also a tribute to her childhood memories. Cupboards and shelves are filled with a variety of whimsical items that include handcrafted wooden toy soliders, Santa Claus figures, miniature china tea sets, and antique teddy bears. Some items are the handiwork of reknowned craftspersons such as Mary Sparger and David Vance, and others are family heirlooms. According to Mary Ann, whether they are valuable or not, they all share a common characteristic because, she says, "Everything in here reminds me of something that makes me happy."

The Allens open the house up in the spring at Easter and live full-time in the mountains until Thanksgiving. During those months, the house is the setting for a round of entertaining traditions. In the summer, typical weekend affairs are casual buffets of fresh fish caught in the shoals, fried and served with hush puppies and cole slaw. A pig roasted over a 240-gallon oil drum for family and friends is a Thanksgiving tradition, and if the weather stays reasonably mild and the roads are passable, Christmas is celebrated with an early afternoon open house in mid-December.

Friends marvel at what the Allens have accomplished, but they acknowledge the home's original rustic construction was in their favor because the cabin's structural unevenness camouflages their trial-and-error renovations. The Allens created a classic country house with its own special character. The result of their efforts is a home that Mary Ann says "has so much history and so much charm, it is just like a comfortable, old sofa."

GEORGIA

Stately Victorian

A GEORGIA MIDTOWN HOUSE

Midtown Atlanta's Phoenixlike recovery from the brink of disastrous neglect within the last ten years has the district functioning at a thriving pace. Located to the north of Atlanta's central business district, the seven-block area borders the city's main thoroughfare, Peachtree, and is filled with an interesting blend of turn-of-the-century mansions and award-winning twentieth century architecture. The neighborhood's mix of offices, museums, performing arts theaters, shops, and restaurants pulses with a vibrant activity balanced by quieter residential streets lined with manicured lawns and lovingly restored homes.

Midtown was still a thickly forested country-

■■■■■■■■■■■■■■■
Wide, wraparound porches and balconies embrace the front and side of this majestic Victorian house situated on a busy corner in one of Midtown Atlanta's urban neighborhoods (above).

■■■■■■■■■■■■■■■
Original cut-lead-glass side windows bracket the home's front door (left).

side in 1846 when the bulk of it was bought for its timber for less than five dollars an acre by the superintendent of the Georgia Railroad, Richard Peters of Pennsylvania. After cutting the timber to fuel production at his nearby flour mill, Peters began subdividing the newly cleared land into small lots for housing in the late 1880s.

The neighborhood's cachet increased with the advent of the mammoth 1881 International Cotton Exposition. Not only did the exposition focus national attention on the city, but the neighborhood benefited from the presence of a newly landscaped park, custom-designed for the exposition, within walking distance from most Midtown residences.

Following the event, the neighborhood experienced a residential boom as an influx of young families moved into the area between 1890 and 1910 and built gabled and gazeboed show

120

homes along Piedmont Avenue. Midtown had made the transition from country cousin to city slicker as the area became home to many of the city's prominent citizens. Their personal and professional successes were reflected in the high-quality buildings they constructed along the streets from brick, stone, marble, and terra-cotta.

By the 1930s, Midtown, though still primarily residential, gained a shopping district. However, the burgeoning commercial growth was quickly stunted as the neighborhood's second generation of well-heeled residents grew up and moved out of the area during the 1950s. This neighborhood exodus marked the beginning of a twenty-year downward slump as businesses faltered and a group of "flower children" adopted the district as their own. Prostitutes, tramps, and drug dealers supplanted the love and peace clique by the 1970s as sleazy establishments

Placed between doors leading into the dining room, a striking Swedish birch Biedermeier secretary, circa 1840, sets the tone for the handsomely decorated home (far left). An Italian papier-mâché bust of the Emperor Constantine looks out across the room. The stairway to the left leads to upstairs bedrooms.

Hollow, oxidized tin finials flank an early nineteenth century English oil painting that graces the entry hall mantel (center). The owners often use the Regency reproduction tripod supper table as a small dining table.

Seen through the library, an old-style contemporary mantel hangs above the entry's working fireplace. The dramatic arrangement of flowers and eucalyptus is an eye-catching display of color and texture (below).

flourished. A length of Peachtree once considered the city's most sought-after address had acquired the unpleasant nickname "The Strip."

Serious attempts to restore houses located in Midtown began in earnest during the late 1970s after the last massage parlor was padlocked. Since then, the neighborhood has upgraded its image in astonishing proportions. Fortune 500 companies have located their headquarters and offices along Peachtree in landmark skyscrapers. Young professionals and families drawn by the neighborhood's promising cultural mix have reclaimed the area and undertaken numerous restoration projects.

Joe Blount and his business associate Luis Garcia were key players in the neighborhood's new vitality. Co-owners of the Atlanta-based Rattanworks reproduction and private design home furnishings firm, Blount first channeled his interests and

■■■■■■■■■■■■■■■■
Spiritual Guatemalan life is evoked in the library's collection of nineteenth century "dressing" saints—figures crafted for religious ceremonies—displayed on a side table (above).

■■■■■■■■■■■■■■■■
A nineteenth century bull's-eye mirror hangs above the library mantel. Small side chairs upholstered in Cowtan & Tout fabric complement the tailored formality of the Victorian chesterfield sofa (right).

■■■■■■■■■■■■■■
The owners' distinctive
accessory collection spans
centuries and continents.
In the den, three late
eighteenth century hand-
tinted shell prints hang
below English fly rods and
a Balinese mask (left).
On the table in front is
a painted carving of a
standing Indian figure. A
large bowl on the coffee
table is filled with
Guatemalan gourds
designed as liquid-chocolate
drinking cups. A sixteenth
century Persian porcelain
vase holds a garden-fresh
bouquet of fresh
hydrangeas.

■■■■■■■■■■■■■■
The den walls are tinted
with a teal-colored base
coat painted over with a
glossy coat of varnish
(right). The owners
upholstered the custom-
made sofa with a Grey
Watkins, Ltd., fabric and
edged it with a Brunschwig
& Fils trim. The
contemporary coffee table
is made of recycled antique
French parquet tiles.
French doors open onto
the back porch.

finances toward the revitalization of a run-down neighborhood
in the early 1980s. Blount became a residential preservationist,
buying older properties in Home Park—a neighborhood adjacent to a college campus—renovating them, and leasing them
back to housing-deprived college students.

Energized by this participation in reclaiming the city's urban
landscape, Blount and Garcia abandoned the serenity of their
suburban residence for the challenge of in-town living in 1985.
In doing so, they took the first step toward earning a "badge of

determination" for salvaging a Midtown Victorian residence
from demolition.

The house was a familiar landmark to the men because it was
on the same street where they lived after first moving to Midtown. Built for $5,000 in 1910, the house was then sold in 1917
to a carriage manufacturer, coincidentally also named Blount.
The structure was divided into eighteen rooms following World
War II to supplement Atlanta's housing shortage. By the 1950s,
the residence was operating as a reputable boardinghouse for

women, but it quickly degenerated as the neighborhood declined during the area's hippie era.

According to Blount, the house was "a nightmare on Fifth and Myrtle" by the time he and Garcia bought it. Though they initially intended to subdivide it into two flats to lease or sell, Blount and Garcia decided to renovate it for themselves.

Their professional instincts for architectural balance and proportion assured them that with work, the house could be a showplace. They turned to architect, Thomas A. Blount, the owner's brother, to help them transform the house into the best they felt it could be. Interior designer Suzanne Allen was enlisted as a member of the collaborative team working to make the structure a home.

The first momentous task in renovating the structure was to clear years of accumulated debris cluttering the house from top to bottom. It took a fleet of city dump trucks to haul off the trash piles. Allen remembers demolition crews working day and night for three weeks before the owners allowed her to set foot inside

A soapstone bowl from Kenya is displayed on the mirrored light mahogany Danish empire console in the hallway connecting the den and kitchen (left). A side kitchen door leads outside to the small garden where the owners grow their cooking herbs.

Ionic columns installed where a wall once stood support a balcony overhang (right). By raising the countertops two or three inches above normal installation height, the owners are able to prepare food at a comfortable level. The side door leads out to a walled herb garden.

A whimsical French carousel pig from the nineteenth century is a centerpiece in the glass-enclosed kitchen breezeway. The back staircase leads to a balcony office area off Joe Blount's bedroom (far right).

the front door for the first time.

After the interior was swept clean, the architect set about restoring the house into its full potential and beyond. "It wasn't a pleasant house at all in the way that it had been divided up. Until we got into the house, we didn't know how much we were going to have to tear out. Because it is a simple house, we didn't want to gussy it up, but we did want to make it a little more finished," says the architect.

Major reconstruction was done on the exterior. It wasn't until the roof was propped up that they all realized more than a fresh coat of paint was required to restore the porches. "It was like pulling a thread on the edge of a sweater. The whole thing began to unravel," says Tom Blount. Replacement columns were

installed along the front, and existing ones that could be salvaged were moved along to the sides. The galleries were rebuilt with weather-treated materials to protect them from the elements.

Inside, the house was stripped down to its skeleton, new electrical wiring and plumbing were installed, Sheetrock was applied, and the floors were braced as the architect undertook the task of eradicating the confusing maze of rooms. The owners sought to create a setting conducive to their quiet life-style. "We never have hundreds of people over, so when we set out to redo this house, we wanted a series of cozy little rooms," says Garcia.

Tom Blount created this intimate environment by organiz-

ing the downstairs interior around the dining room. He describes the original dining room as "an asymmetrical room with no focus where nothing lined up with anything." To solve this space problem, he opened up a narrow corridor connecting the original dining room with the atrium and created a sense of order by lining up doors, passageways, and windows along a cross axis.

Rather than place the dining room off by itself, as is done in traditional floor plans, Tom Blount incorporated the room into a working space by enlarging the openings and routing traffic from the front to the back directly through both ends of the room. For formal dinners, the pocket and paneled doors installed in the four openings are closed.

While rebuilding the back half of the house, Joe Blount and Luis Garcia were able to examine the structure of a separate building that had previously been moved onto the lot and attached to the original house as a kitchen expansion. Already rotting, the back wall enclosing the left side of the first and second floors was removed. The exisiting rooms were built to match the older, still structurally sound addition's shape and dimensions. Where the old wall was torn out to connect the kitchen and den, two Ionic columns were inserted for support on either end of the cooking island. The rear addition and reshuffling of downstairs spaces dictated changes in the layout of upstairs rooms. One bedroom was lost to make room for two baths and four closets, the master bedroom was enlarged and

Cushioned wicker easy chairs upholstered in hand-loomed fabrics from Guatemala are clustered in a sheltered courtyard porch off the contemporary kitchen (left).

The owners unwind on a small porch overlooking a back courtyard's potted garden (above).

gained a balcony, and a loftlike office was added overlooking the kitchen.

Finishing touches contribute to the light and easy elegance of the interior. Low-voltage, recessed lighting softly illuminates artwork hanging above fireplaces and over sofas and bookcase vignettes. Wide molding borders were added above the doorways, and plantation shutters were hung across the windows.

Rather than stain hardwood floors dark, the owners broke from tradition and applied a thin coat of white paint cut with mineral spirits to veil the wood grain with a pale wash of color. To create the glossy, textured finish of the crimson-colored walls in the library, a deep magenta was applied with a rag over a base coat of pink. Then the paint was covered with a topcoat of varnish to give the walls a rich, leathery look.

The interior's elegant, restrained furnishings are representative of the owners' professional interests and personal tastes as knowledgeable antique and home furnishings authorities and collectors. They were among the first Southern dealers to import Biedermeier furniture. They bought many of the pieces for themselves. A Swedish Biedermeier secretary placed in the entry was purchased during a trip to Brighton, England. This and other prize pieces, such as the master bedroom's Philippine altar table, are mixed with custom-designed upholstered pieces and Victorian chairs and sofas. The owners restored many of the antique upholstered items.

Diverse religious and eclectic collections complement the house's classical decor. Garcia infused the residence with the spirit of his native land of Guatemala by decorating tabletops and bookcases with native handcrafted objects. Guatemalan *santos* perch in library bookshelf niches, gourd cups and bowls adorn the coffee table. A traditional Guatemalan wedding garment called a *huipil* hangs on a back stairway landing.

When entertaining, the homeowners enjoy hosting small dinners rather than large receptions. Two round dining room folding tables draped with patterned fabric seat fourteen guests. The entry's tripod table can seat up to four more people.

Most evenings, though, friends and guests lounge in the den at the back of the house, the homeowners' favorite room, or perch on stools pulled up to the kitchen island counter and watch as final meal preparations are made.

The owners installed sleek Euro-style American appliances in the roomy kitchen; stretches of Corian countertops provide attractive and serviceable working areas for cutting and chopping. A collection of international cookbooks lines built-in shelving,

and a vignette of colorful wooden Guatemalan figures breaks up the room's pristine whiteness. A small porch off the kitchen overlooks a shady brick courtyard. Enclosed by an open fence, the space serves as both a romping area for the household's three miniature schnauzers and a setting for warm-weather meals and parties.

The owners trusted their instincts and took a gamble on a neighborhood and a house others had written off as lost causes. They reap a daily reward simply living within the home's graceful spaciousness that they now proudly call home.

■■■■■■■■■■■■■
Luis's upstairs bedroom opens on to the front balcony overlooking a busy avenue lined with oak trees (left). The room's interior is a composition in soft neutrals. Fabrics by Grey Watkins, Ltd., decorate the bed.

■■■■■■■■■■■■■■
The master bedroom opens on to a gallery overlooking the back, brick courtyard (above). The owners expanded the size of the room and added the porch. The bed is draped in yards of neutral linens by Hinson & Company.

Pastoral Retreat

AN APPALACHIAN FOOTHILLS FARM IN GEORGIA

Agriculture has played a significant role in Georgia's history since the state's beginnings as the last of America's original thirteen colonies. Bartow County, tucked away in the state's northwest corner near the Tennessee border, boasts a lengthy agricultural pedigree that can be traced directly back to the Cherokee people. These Native Americans prospered on the fertile uplands prior to the arrival of white settlers. The Indians cleared productive farms from the wooded highlands, and—according to Lucy Cunyus, who wrote *History of Bartow County*—cultivated corn patches on the land before conquistador Hernando de Soto traveled through the area in 1540 exploring for gold.

133

■■■■■■■■■■■■■■
A handcrafted rocker sits on the front patio just outside the screened-porch door. The present owners painted the structure's original exterior blue gray in the mid 1980's (below).

■■■■■■■■■■■■■■
The main room's exposed pine beams run above an open-hearth fireplace built with stones collected from the property (above).

The owners whitewashed the kitchen's original cabinets before tiling the counters and bricking the floors (far left). A reproduction cookstove works with electricity.

A small stoop leads from the main room into an open-air dining porch (left).

The screened porch's solid pine table is constructed from the same timber used to build the house (below). A large painting by black American folk artist Sam Doyle hangs on the back wall over an arrangement of freshly cut wheat grown on the farm's acreage. The owners bought the small green wall lamps and the large glass storage jar in France.

lookout for a new tract of land suitable for his cattle and a family weekend home.

In 1971, he bought acreage across the fence from the Calico Valley farm and hired an architect to draw preliminary plans for a contemporary residence complete with tennis courts and a swimming pool. But construction plans for the proposed getaway estate stopped the moment Falk first saw the neighboring cabin and surrounding fields.

Because the structure and lake are hidden by the hilly terrain, Falk was unaware of the cabin's presence until he began walking his own property. He encountered the rustic building on one of his strolls and was completely seduced by its setting. Falk estimates he has brokered the sale of more than seventy thousand acres during his career, but contends the Calico Valley farm

■■■■■■■■■■■■■■■
Glints of early morning sunlight cast a warm glow on the master bedroom's pine-paneled walls (left). Antique linens make the brass bed an inviting resting place.

■■■■■■■■■■■■■■■
Howard Finster's *Tree of Life* sculpture stands by the window in a corner of the bathroom and is covered with colorful hatpins (near right).

■■■■■■■■■■■■■■■
Imported Italian tiles and sink basin lend a charming touch to the bathroom (far right). The room is only large enough to accommodate the sink and shower.

property "is, for its size, the prettiest I've ever seen."

Determined to own the cabin and property, Falk spent the next eight months making friends with Raines until the gentleman farmer was convinced Falk would make a good neighbor and relented in 1972 by selling him two hundred acres and the house. Today, the men are very close friends and Raines is the manager of Falk's cabin and property.

The cabin plays country cousin to the Falks' sophisticated city residence. The Falks flee the city most spring and summer weekends for the cabin's sanctuary of simple pleasures. Because

there are no telephones, radios, or televisions in the house, contact with the outside world is limited to the occasional neighbor strolling down the country lane. The Falks spend many afternoons lolling in the airy embrace of hammocks hung among the stand of dogwoods, maples, pines, and cottonwoods. Wash Falk recently bought a small rowboat and banked it alongside the lake for his early evening fishing expeditions.

A continual progression of seasonal dramas color and change the scenic vistas surrounding the cabin. Spring's young grasses dance beneath cool breezes until summer's harvest transforms

the hills into a closely cropped terrain. The Falks were married in 1978 on the crest of one of these gentle hills with a view of the mist-ringed mountains and their cabin nestled snugly below them among the trees.

Washed in a pale slate blue, the cabin practically disappears at a distance against the expanse of sky. Constructed entirely from pine timber cleared off the land, the modest-sized building contains five rooms, including a screened porch that functions as an open-air dining room. The exterior's horizontal boards are worked in a clapboard pattern supported by an uncut rubble foundation. A stone chimney built with rocks collected on the property stands at the back of the house.

Few alterations were needed to make the cabin suitable for the Falks' uncomplicated weekend life-style. They maintained the structure's simple interior, choosing to do no more than upgrade the working areas. Judy bricked over the kitchen's floor and tiled the countertops before whitewashing the room's existing walls and cabinets. More tile work was done in the cabin's only bathroom, where a glass-walled shower was installed.

The couple made a conscious decision to let the interior of

■■■■■■■■■■■■■
An Atlanta decorative
artist stenciled and painted
a series of delicate floral
patterns on the bunk
room's hardwood
floor (left).

■■■■■■■■■■■■■
Two sets of bunk beds in
the guest bedroom are
fitted with down-filled
mattresses and heirloom
quilts. Heavy chains
support the weight of
the top two bunks (right).

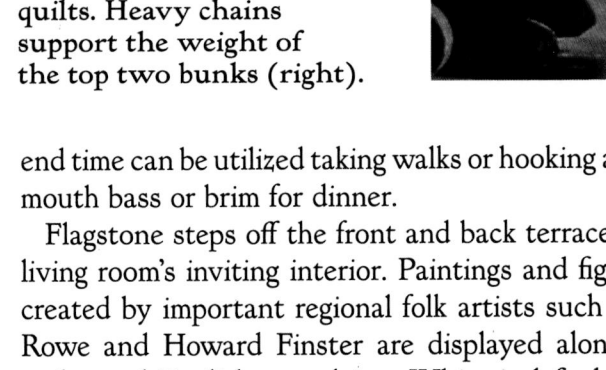

this house be a complete departure from their city home's pristine starkness. Their snug cottage exudes a well-worn charm.
The furnishings are an eclectic mixture of new and old that
offsets a colorful collection of folk art and crafts. Paneled and
floored throughout in the same richly colored pine planks, the
house requires nothing more than a quick sweep and dusting.
Low maintenance is important to the Falks so that their week-

end time can be utilized taking walks or hooking a catch of large-
mouth bass or brim for dinner.

Flagstone steps off the front and back terraces lead into the
living room's inviting interior. Paintings and figurative objects
created by important regional folk artists such as Nellie Mae
Rowe and Howard Finster are displayed alongside heirloom
quilts and English porcelains. Whimsical finds decorate sur-

142

faces and nooks, and a collection of baskets hangs along the porch's ceiling.

The cottage's small rooms are Spartan. A deep, soft sofa is placed invitingly before the open-hearth fireplace, and rocking chairs are pulled up to its sides. Tables and chairs were brought out of storage and arranged as an eating area in the great room. The extra bedroom is furnished with two sets of built-in bunk beds. The back room's paneled interior is softened by a delicate floral border hand-painted across the floor.

A brass bed, a washstand, and a wooden bench are the master bedroom's sole contents. But for the Falks, the tiny room is a wealth of luxuries. Here they can awaken as gentle breezes carry the rhythmic whirring sounds of a lakeside bullfrog's morning tune in through the cabin's open windows and doors.

Marshside Manor

A GEORGIA RIVERFRONT ESTATE

Wide columned porches stretching across fronts of stately homes are a classic hallmark of southern living. Their open yet protected expanses, so often furnished with deep-cushioned wicker rockers and comfortable swings, emanate an air of gentle hospitality closely associated with the region. These gracious spaces invite languid afternoon visits with family or friends.

Inspired by these romantic images, childhood memories, and the compelling beauty of a large white porch, one couple spent several years renovating a Georgian-style house into a waterfront retreat large enough for their family of five children.

■■■■■■■■■■■■■■
Morning sunlight streams across the water onto the front of the house and gently warms the spacious expanse of the porch's elegantly rounded curves (above). The central doorway opens on to the main hallway and is original to the house.

■■■■■■■■■■■■■■
Perched on a high thirty-three-foot bluff above a saltwater river, the home is surrounded by a vivid summer setting (left). Bright blue water and sky meet the sparkling greens of the lawn and marsh grasses.

■■■■■■■■■■■■■■■

A majestic oak dripping with Spanish moss frames a stunning view of the tidal river and salt marsh expanse stretching out beyond the house (center). The low concrete steps on the right lead into the glass-enclosed sun-porch addition.

■■■■■■■■■■■■■■

Fresh shrimp caught from the river in seine nets are just one saltwater delicacy brought in by the tides (below). The waterway's other bountiful delights include crab and flounder.

■■■■■■■■■■■■■■■

The property's original drive wound around to the left side of the house but was redesigned during the renovation to align it with the front entrance (far right). Airy iron columns that complement the design of an already existing iron gate and a newly installed iron picket fence were substituted for the entrance's original brick pillars.

After seeing the property for the first time, the wife was instantly attracted to the house by its expansive porch. It evoked her fond memories of growing up in a nearby rural farming community. "The riverfront porch brings back memories of the wonderful times we spent on my grandfather's porch," she explains. "Where ours has so many curves, his was square. He lived near my parents' house, so I could walk right down the road where I spent many an afternoon and weekend with my cousins, aunts, and uncles."

The glamor of her new porch stretching along the riverfront of the house is matched by the panorama of unblemished salt marshes that unfolds before it. Located along a coastal Georgia area, the house is perched on a thirty-three-foot bluff overlooking a tranquil tidal river and a pastoral expanse of trees and un-

disturbed marshlands. A manicured lawn rolls out just beyond a clipped hedge that borders the house nestled beneath spectacular live oaks dripping with Spanish moss. The lush grass reaches to the water's edge, where a weathered dock juts out over the river.

On the road entrance at the back of the house, wild cherries, dogwoods, magnolias, and more majestic oaks shade the shell-lined driveway. Inside, gleaming Georgia pine floorboards and polished antiques match the owners' gracious life-style. On one side of the house, large single-paned windows frame views of stately trees, and on the other, shimmering reflections bounce up off the sunlit waterway.

In 1977 the owners happened upon the house while visiting a friend living next door. When they saw the shingled struc-

ture, they were immediately struck by its dramatic views and secluded setting. "We looked over and saw those beautiful oak trees and thought how glorious that was." They were even more delighted when they saw a FOR SALE sign tacked up at the front gate.

The discovery was timely since they were searching for more space for their expanding family. "We saw the house with its trees and came to the conclusion that we would be happier having our children out on the river exploring and sailing in a boat than playing on the street. Since moving here we have all developed a healthy respect for the water and are comforted by it at the same time."

The saltwater river running alongside the house ebbs and swells with the sea tides and has for centuries served as a path-

■■■■■■■■■■■■■■■
A pair of gently curved
arches frame the original
back entry and bracket
where the former staircase
led up to the second floor
(left). The hallway's open,
flowing space runs the
width of the house and
separates the dining and
living rooms. All five
children enjoyed rides in
the baby pram now parked
in the corner.

■■■■■■■■■■■■■■■
The handrail on the
staircase in the entry hall
was at one time salvaged
from an old hospital (right).

way for both trade and pleasure. Accounts indicate that the bluff was a favorite camping ground for migrating Indians, such as native Creeks and Cherokees, who conducted casual trade by selling crafts and skins from their canoes. The French landed during the Revolutionary War, and the Spanish frequently traveled the river on missionary voyages up from Florida to out-lying sea islands and north into the Carolinas. The notorious pirate Blackbeard also left his mark on the area by burying a chest filled with gold coins and a sword that was found and car-ried off to the Civil War by a Confederate officer.

The land's fertile soil supported a number of colonial planta-tions during the 1700s that were later subdivided into smaller lots. By the 1800s this gradual development led to the area's

transformation into a resort community. People escaped from the sweltering summer heat and bouts of malaria, retreating to the hotels and vacation homes built along the bluff where they could enjoy the gently cooling tidal breezes.

While researching their home's history the couple discovered that the house was built in 1906 as a summer home during the area's resort boom by Joseph Chestnutt, who came to the area from Wilmington, North Carolina. Designed as a secondary residence, the original structure was a simple configuration of three rooms lined up side by side on the first and second floors. A small L-shaped wing extending off the first-floor dining room toward the road contained a small kitchen, a sitting room, and a tiny breakfast nook.

■■■■■■■■■■■■■■■■
The formal dining room is illuminated by the warm glow of candlelight shining down from an antique chandelier (above). Informal evening meals and gala holiday affairs are celebrated around the banquet-sized table.

■■■■■■■■■■■■■■
An archway designed as a balanced transition between existing and added areas connects a front sitting area to the original living room (right). Both rooms are furnished with a complementary mixture of English antiques and reproductions.

This original design did not offer enough living space to house the current owners' family; but, fascinated with historical structures and determined to make the house fit their needs, the owners carefully renovated to maintain the structure's balance and elegant riverfront proportions. "We came to the house and tried to let it dictate to us what to do. We didn't want to create something; we just needed space and something we could enjoy."

By working with an architect, they achieved their goal by squaring off the back of the house so that it was even with the kitchen wing. They jokingly recall that "whatever wall we didn't knock down, we moved." During the construction they were also able to alter the back's unattractive façade by installing windows inset into deep white casings and adding a small,

rounded portico entrance bracketed by four columns that echoes the grand front porch.

Repairs to the original porch were also made. A variety of Corinthian and Doric capitals topped the fourteen columns when the home owners acquired the house. They suspect that limited accessibility to architectural details when the house was built may have dictated the mismatched combination of capitals or that damaged ones were haphazardly replaced over the years with no concern for consistency. Ever conscious of the smallest detail, they replaced the older capitals with Doric ones.

A glassed-in porch wing lined with French doors was built along the left side of the house adjacent to the kitchen and the dining room. This elongated room, furnished with white wicker, supports the second-floor master bedroom's spacious

balcony and balances the two-story addition on the opposite end of the house. The family pauses for leisurely lunches in this sun-filled room at a table overlooking the river during busy summer weekdays.

In the opposite wing a first-floor music room runs the entire length of the addition beneath the bedrooms on the second floor. This climate-controlled room is not a feature ordinarily found in homes, but it symbolizes the family's passion for music. A trained classical pianist, the mother encouraged each of her children to develop a musical talent, and the family quintet grew to include two pianos and three cellos. The room's sizable dimensions are perfect as a stage area for practice sessions and impromptu family concerts for holiday and summer gatherings.

When the room was built, special considerations were made to protect the instruments from exposure to the damp air rolling in off the surrounding marshes. The owners connected the living room and the addition with a small corridor, installing large pocket doors to shut off, cool, or heat the music room separately as needed.

Softly curved archways, identically shaped like the new back entrance, serve as pleasing transitions between old and new spaces. An unobstructed view through to porch and river is framed inside the entrance by a pair of arches installed where the original door once stood. A single archway gracefully connects the original living room and a new front seating area with a fireplace.

The back doors and the mantels surrounding the downstairs fireplaces were designed by the architect and handcrafted in

The combination of columns, live oaks, and a collection of wicker furniture makes a delightful backdrop for al fresco dining on the front porch (below).

After an unsuccessful attempt at pickling the sun-porch floors, the owners painted a marine design of waves and fish across the hardwood floors (center). French doors open out over the yard.

Kentucky. He detailed the music room's and the living room's two mantels with the same formal, scallop design and left the entry-hall and dining-room mantels plain. One-piece moldings were copied from an existing original window and enlarged to bracket the downstairs doorway. The home owners requested that pineapple medallions, traditional symbols of southern hospitality, be added in the top two corners of the doorway moldings. Downstairs, the original floors were removed and replaced with native Georgia heart-of-pine boarding. The rooms are filled with their golden glow.

The spectacular sights and sounds of the surroundings contribute to the home's rich character. The couple intentionally left the downstairs windows bare of curtains to allow unrestricted views of the magnificent setting. The mood of each room lightens and darkens with the sun's changing positions. Shutters and curtains are hung across bedroom windows for privacy.

Since the house is closed up only during the dead calm of summer's heat and the height of winter's cold, light breezes waft in through doors and windows throughout most of the year. A chorus of sounds is carried in by these free-flowing breezes.

"Living here, you are very much in touch with what is going on outside since the house is open so much of the year and you are constantly walking by these windows," admit the owners. "It is our creature comfort to hear so many friends out here. You can hear sounds in the marsh grass—birds and marsh hens—and we see fireflies during the summer. We can even look out and see deer that come off the islands and swim over looking for food or water standing and grazing in the yard."

The family's five children have spent much of their playtime in this tree fort located just beyond the driveway's edge (below).

The unrestricted manner in which the family lives in their house is an extension of the carefree life-style the bluff provides its residents. Prize orchids grown in one garden are objects of beauty shared with all and displayed in parlor bouquets. A neighboring vineyard supplies a summer harvest of garden-fresh grapes. Lawns are crisscrossed with paths where children take shortcuts to reach neighboring docks for sailing adventures. And boats motoring by carry passengers who wave and shout greetings.

Year round, the family celebrates the house and its setting with open-air dinners. During the cooler winter months this means backyard oyster roasts, a coastal tradition. Hearty buffets of ham and red rice are enjoyed with the bushels of fresh oysters steamed in open pits beneath croker sacks. In the sum-

mer evening parties are held on the grassy front lawn running alongside the river.

Still, with all the modifying and enlarging, the porch remains the family's favorite spot for entertaining during the spring, summer, and fall. For luncheons, or even an informal dinner, guests are invited to sit around a large round table arranged with floral-patterned china and polished silver.

On quieter evenings husband and wife retreat to the luxury of their open-air room, where they enjoy one another's company, relax in the grandeur of the landscape, and listen to nature's delicate chirps and whispers, the sweet, mellow sounds of a son's or daughter's solo cello, and the soft, lapping noise of the river's gentle current.

155

FLORIDA

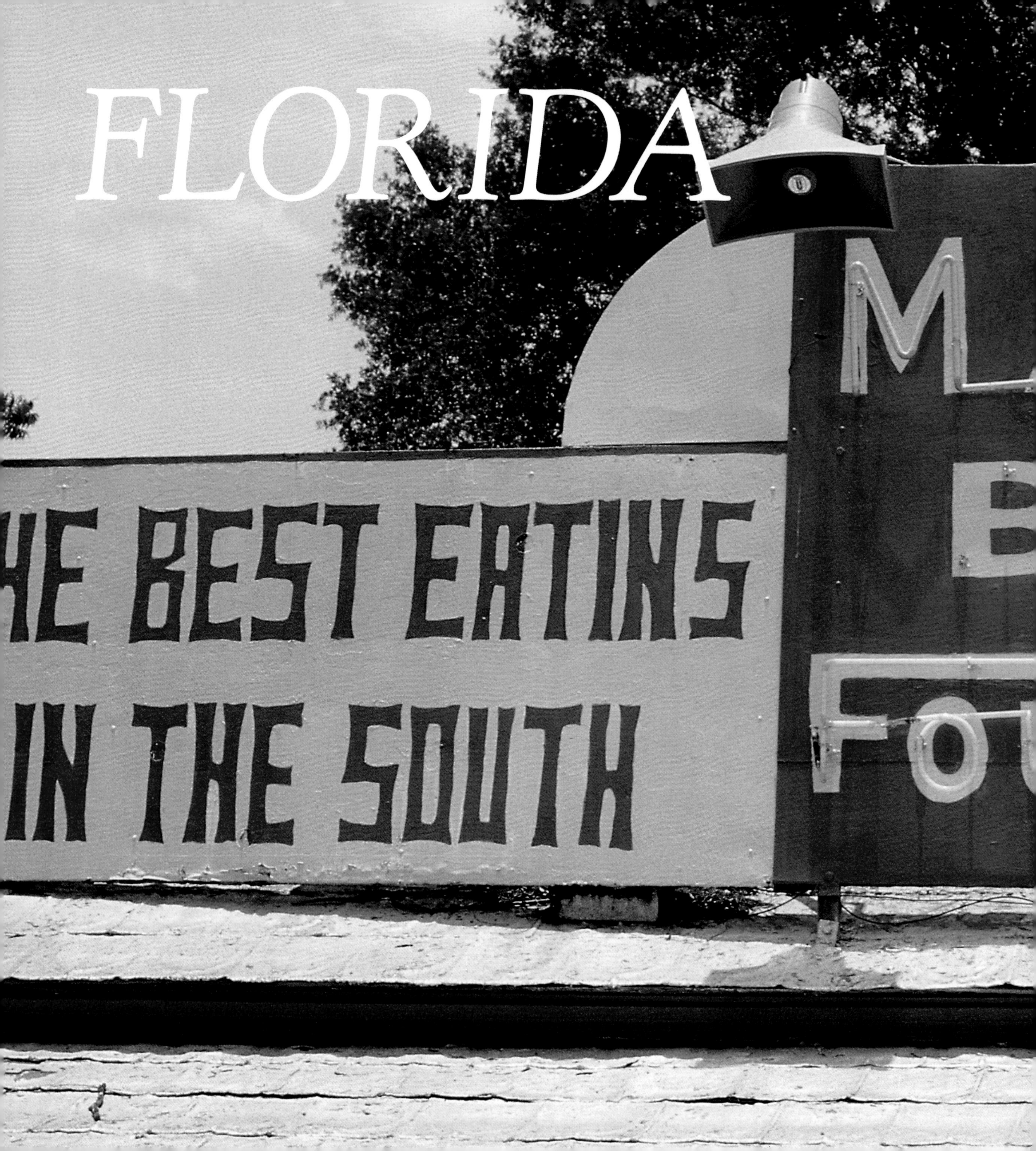

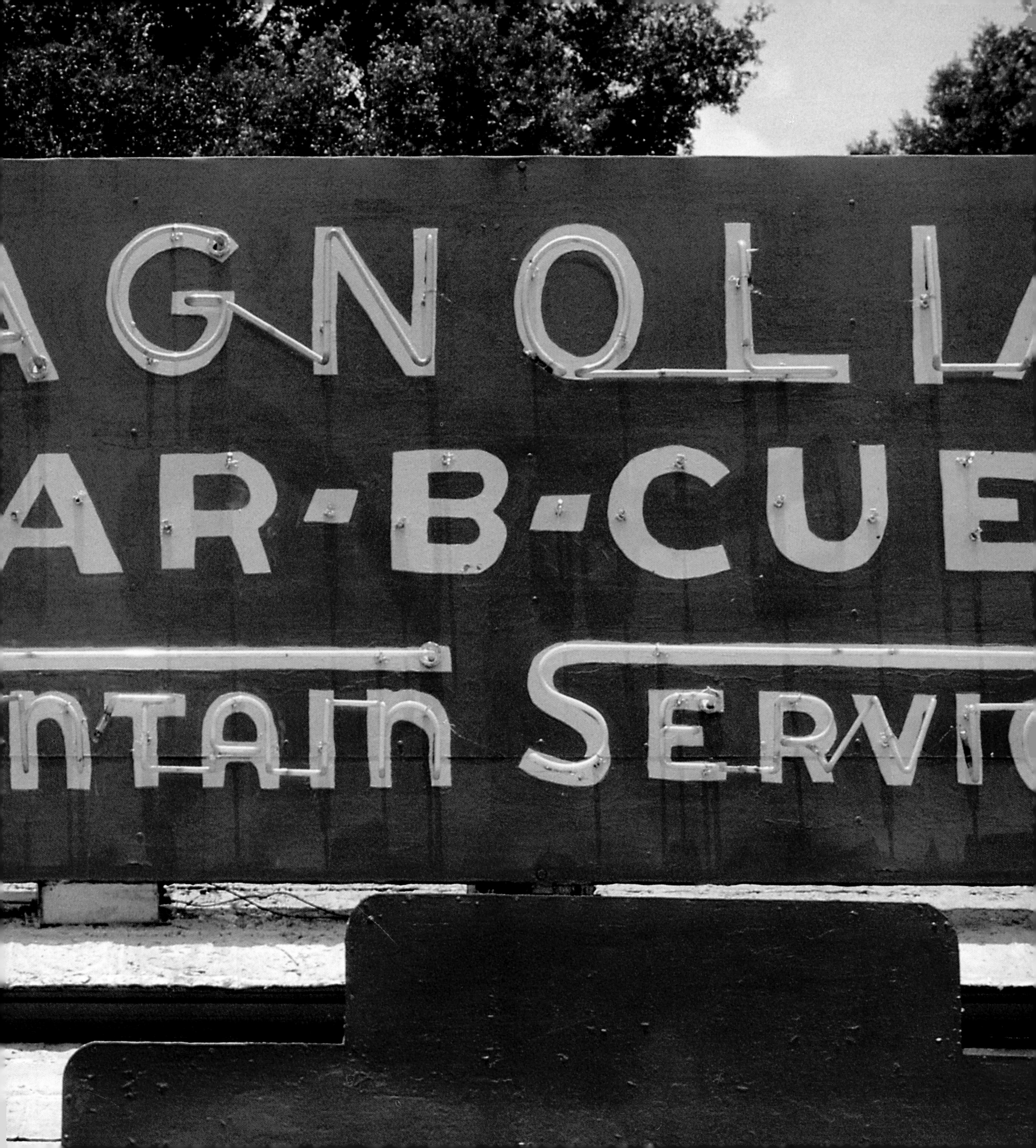
AGNOLI
AR-B-CUE
NTAIN SERVI

Seashore Original

A CONTEMPORARY FLORIDA BEACH HOUSE

Jacksonville offers its growing population an advantage most other major southern cities can't—oceanfront living. Only the intra-coastal waterways separate a commuter from the downtown district. A stretch of residential areas collectively referred to as the "Beaches" hugs the shore. Atlantic Beach is one of these neighborhoods. Originally established in the 1920s as a summer community, the district now attracts people who want to live outside the uniformity of planned suburban communities.

Longtime Atlantic Beach residents enjoy the life-style this seashore haven affords them. Back-yard swimming pools are community property, neighborhood potluck dinners are still a week-

A lush tangle of honeysuckle, wisteria, and trumpet vines shades the backyard pergola, a verdant corridor running perpendicular to the house where the homeowner takes her morning breakfast and enjoys afternoon breaks (left). A row of six Adirondack chairs faces out across the floral-bordered courtyard.

A play of light and texture lends a whimsical charm to this Atlantic Beach house, which was built on the homeowner's childhood property (above). Its design is based on a variety of regional architectural styles. A tower belvedere accesses the sights and sounds of the Florida coastline community.

159

■ ■ ■ ■ ■ ■ ■ ■ ■ ■ ■ ■
This concrete block wing forms the entry courtyard and contains the homeowner's art studio and garage. Architect Steven Harris chose the common material as an affectionate reference to the type of bungalows that cropped up across Florida after World War II (below).

■ ■ ■ ■ ■ ■ ■ ■ ■ ■ ■ ■
The main living area incorporates seating, dining, and cooking areas (above). With a Carmen Miranda flair, the homeowner uses vivid colors to unite the room's mix of art, inherited furnishings, and junk-sale finds.

end happening, and the life-style is described as "easy" and "laid back." In short, the quaint residential area fosters the sorts of friendships that last a lifetime. The spirit of one neighborhood friendship is celebrated in the first house designed by architect Steven Harris.

Harris traces his relationship with the homeowner back to his own childhood. It was inevitable that their families' histories would become closely knit, since both were raised in the small Atlantic Beach community. Though the architect and client share several connections, their most significant one is his aunt's close friendship with the homeowner.

This mutual tie brought Harris and his client together during family outings, and as early as 1975 the two had begun a casual dialogue about houses and gardens. A ceramicist and local high school art teacher, the homeowner was living in her childhood house when she and Harris began planning her new house. The rambling size of the older house, in a neighborhood originally built in the 1920s, and the aging structure's state of decline forced her to consider other alternatives.

She did not have to look any farther than her own backyard to find a suitable location for the new structure. Harris quartered off a back portion of the lot—approximately 125-by-50

Fringe trim and rainbow colors transform the 1950s Choco-ware lamps into eye-catching decorative statements. A plywood and canvas mural of the homeowner's three sons by artist Lucien Rees-Roberts (left).

Artist Michael Davis's purple basket is prominently displayed beside the door leading out to the pergola (above).

feet—to be the site for the new home before the original house and yard were sold.

From the outset, the owner gave Harris three primary guidelines. She specifically requested a great room with areas for living, dining, and cooking. She asked that the house be designed so the front door could not be viewed from the street. Finally, she required that the house contain only two bedrooms, one separated from the main house with its own entry as guest quarters for visits from her three adult sons.

The client felt comfortable giving Harris total freedom of design because she herself never relinquishes creative control of her work to anyone else. "Why would I have the audacity to tell an architect how to design a house?" says the artist. "Just as I don't want anyone to tell me how to make a pot, I would not begin to try and tell him what should be done."

The dynamics of this partnership are reflected in the way the house resonates with a singular identity dictated only by Harris's architectural interests and familiarity with his client's lifestyle and needs. Using an interrelated arrangement of structures, he designed a living compound that represents a number of building types—including post–World War II bungalows.

The structure's link with historical references begins with the asbestos-shingled roof. Harris chose this type of roofing after he discovered the material was widely used in southern residential structures. The shingles' toxic properties make the products hard to find, but the supply problem was solved when one of the homeowner's former neighbors sold his stockpile of salvaged asbestos shingles to her as a favor.

A now-demolished local landmark was the inspiration for the roof's turquoise color. The nearby 1940s-vintage Bennett's Motel had what Harris calls "the most beautiful roof I've ever seen." Painting the shingles a blue green was also an affordable way to mimic the appearance of more expensive copper roofing.

In designing the house, Harris incorporated pieces of two postwar housing styles. The concrete-block corridor linking the main room to the owner's studio represents nondescript ranch houses that popped up across Florida after World War II. The main living area's Mediterranean-influenced stucco exterior echoes the architectural style popularized after World War I.

Through research, Harris learned that Mediterranean architecture was first introduced to the state around 1914. Apparently, the south of France was a popular vacation destination for Americans prior to that time, but at the war's outbreak travel to the area was halted. Americans intent on capturing the charm of the French coast simply duplicated in burgeoning

■■■■■■■■■■■■■■■■
Artist Ken Hatcher's
Winged Victory sculpture
stands guard at the
stairwell entrance. A
Seminole Indian dress,
given to the homeowner
by a family friend, hangs
framed along a sheet metal
wall above a thread
display case filled with
multicolored wooden
spools (left).

■■■■■■■■■■■■■■■
The homeowner
upholstered a corner
rocking chair with her
own dye-painted and
quilted fabric. The chair's
colors reflect the same
vibrant oranges and reds
found in the garden's
zinnia border (right).

■■■■■■■■■■■■■■■
A coverlet hand-quilted by
the homeowner is draped
across the corner of a
wicker sofa, beside a chair
slipcovered in durable bed-
ticking fabric (far right).

Florida resort communities the Mediterranean-style villas they had seen on their European coastal jaunts.

The lot's location three blocks from the beach left the house without an ocean view. Harris cleverly resolved this dilemma by constructing a thirty-five-foot-tall retreat similar to industrial watchtowers used as lookout posts by southern pine forest rangers. The metal structure supports a third-floor belvedere atop the tower that offers uninterrupted blue and green vistas of treetops and skies.

The tower also functions as the homeowner's secluded perch. She says, "I can go up on the third floor and look out and see people drive by. I can tell by their shocked reactions that they often just can't believe this house. I even had one man ask me if it was a church."

When fitting these diverse building components together, Harris held two ideas foremost in mind. The first he lists as the "light industrial surface yards" seen across the southeast within fenced areas, where many small tradesmen live and work. Not-

164

ing that northeastern versions of these compounds are called "agrian farmyards," Harris says he was struck by the pragmatic, yet deliberately informal relationships between the residential and storage structures inside these complexes. Harris delegated similarly separate functions to each of the house's components.

Harris's second idea was to pay tribute to the arrangement of large neighborhood beach houses on their lots. "I love Atlantic Beach," Harris says. "The houses and the way they sit on their property is fairly regular. The big houses along the ocean sit

with the main house facing the sea, and behind the house is a garden, and along the street is a two-story garage apartment. There is this kind of three-layering affair going on."

He drew on this same formula as he pieced the owner's house together. A gray structure fronting the house contains a garage and guest quarters and serves as the foreground. Behind this is a one-story corridor that holds a pottery studio and connects the garage and main living wing. The third architectural element is a garden space located in the back, accessible from the living quarters through French doors.

In his choice of materials, Harris paid homage to "three histories of architecture" in northern Florida. For this reason, the compound is whimsically dressed beneath a multilayered coat of galvanized steel, concrete block, stucco, and cedar—all materials that, at the owner's request, will require low maintenance or none at all.

The intricate but straightforward design blushes with the homeowner's "insane" love of color. Her fondness for bold colors dictated the intensity of the exterior's ocher-tinted stucco. Harris chose the mustard shade from his memories of the similarly stained stucco bungalows dotting Italy's Tuscany region. More pigment was added at the homeowner's urgings until the stucco mixture turned a richer mustard shade.

Color was also used to revitalize the original monochromatic interior. The wall surfaces were initially painted cream as a neutral backdrop that would complement the owner's art collection. Yet, after moving in, she gradually began infusing the rooms with her own personality by using vivid layers of paint. She admits her eye for pattern and texture is forceful, saying, "Everywhere I've lived has always been a little peculiar, because I've always painted everything."

Her uninhibited painting transforms the character of walls as well as lamps and tables, creating a Technicolor wave of peacock blues, apple greens, rosy purples, and bright yellows that extends across the entire living area, stopping only at doorway and window moldings and the room's twelve-foot ceiling. A wall of sheet metal where the stair tower intrudes is the room's only large block of neutral color.

A collection of arts and crafts that the owner acquired through trades with artist friends remains the home's decorative focus. A large plywood and canvas portrait of her sons by Lucien Rees-Roberts rests above the fireplace. A ceramic platter from her own *Killer Ducks* series dominates a side table. The stairwell and the bathroom walls are covered with artwork. In the kitchen, Harris designed open-air shelving as a display area for pottery, colored glass, and smaller objects, such as her sons' sterling baby mugs.

Placed within these art-filled walls is a comfortable mixture of inherited and junk-store furnishings ideally suited to the owner's casual life-style. Durable upholsteries and indestructible tile floors invite her family of sons, friends, and her beloved dogs to lounge freely about the house.

Conversations between architect and client led Harris to ex-

166

■■■■■■■■■■■■■■■
A cluster of framed zinnias and a trio of old postcards picturing Atlantic Beach and the neighboring Neptune Beach community hang along the stairway leading up to the second-floor bedroom and bath (above). A silver box salvaged from a trash pile now serves as a stairwell display shelf.

■■■■■■■■■■■■■■■
Glass blocks inset across the kitchen's tiled back wall illuminate the marble countertops and the open shelf displays of cobalt-blue-rimmed glassware and pottery (near right).

■■■■■■■■■■■■■■■
A border of tiles decorated with the owner's own *Spike* dog figures dances in the kitchen (far right).

tend the home's living space outside. Shocked at the way many contemporary houses are sited with no relation to their landscape, Harris created an even balance between house and garden so the areas complement each other.

The outdoor room's contents are both decorative and functional in their design. The owner uses a black lap pool that lines up with the front door for therapeutic exercise. Harris describes the gleaming reflecting pool as "a horizontal mirror that looks as if a slice of sky has been dropped into the ground." A pergola covered in a fragrant tangle of honeysuckle, wisteria, and trumpet vines is another Mediterranean design import Harris interpreted with a southern twist. His memories of south Georgia hunting lodges built of rough-hewn logs during the 1930s inspired him to use rustic wood columns.

Ironically, though the owner rebelled when the shaded sanctuary was erected, she now claims it is her favorite space. She spends part of every day eating and reading beneath its lush cover. "Down here, a pergola is so soothing," she says, "because we can live outside so much. Many of my friends are building one."

The owner has even brought the charm of her beloved garden and its pergola inside. An elaborate design she painted across her bedroom ceiling echoes the leafy green foliage on the banana trees and elephant ears growing beside the garden structure. Unfazed by the owner's change of heart, Harris remarks, "It seems to me with almost every house there is something a client doesn't ask for, doesn't have any use for, but once they have it, they can't live without it."

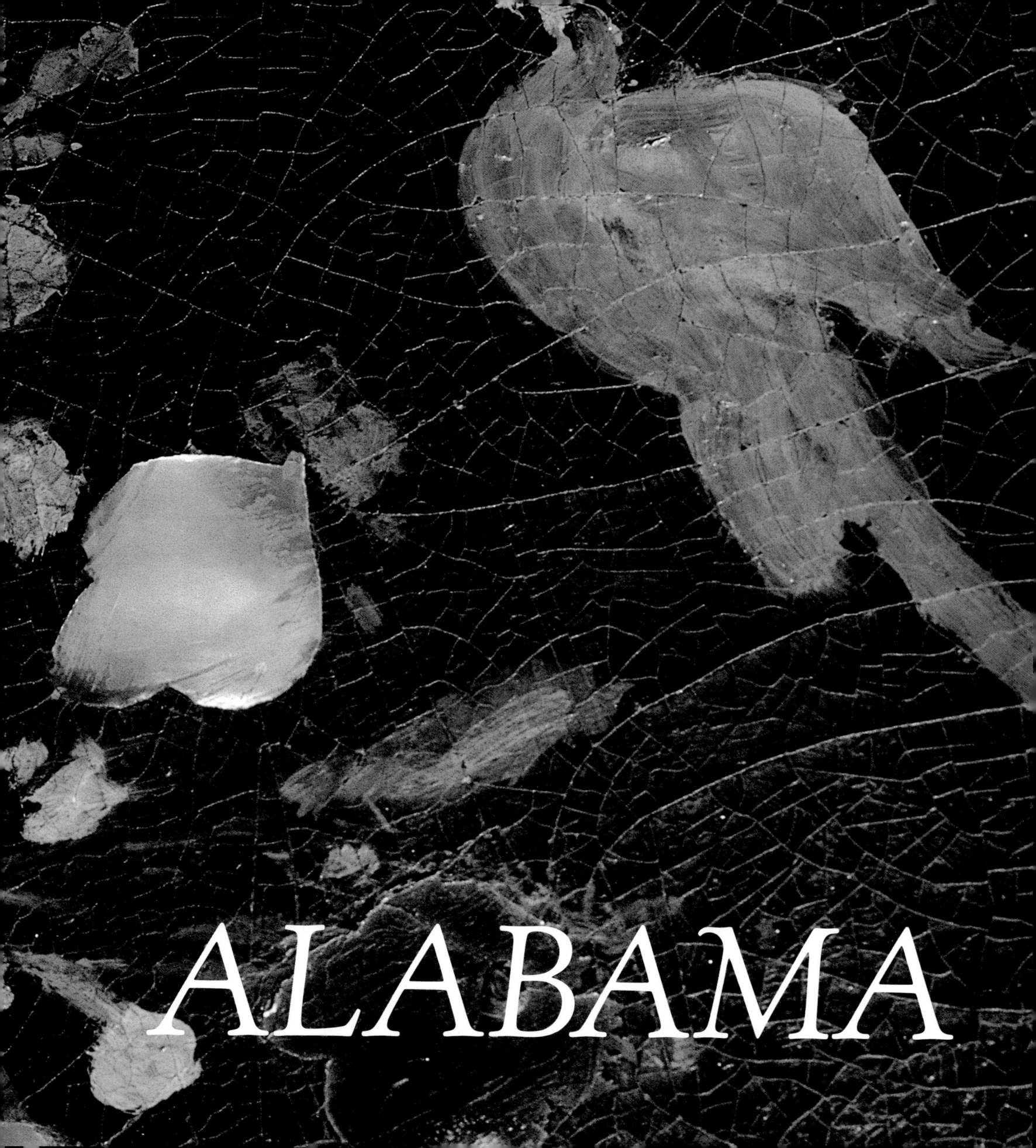

ALABAMA

Southern Ancestry

AN ALABAMA FAMILY HOME

■■■■■■■■■■■■■■■■
The Greek Revival–style house constructed entirely of native Alabama heart of pine boasts a full-height porch (above). This architectural style was first popularized in Philadelphia after the War of 1812. The tradition spread to New York during the 1820s but didn't reach the Deep South until fifteen years later.

■■■■■■■■■■■■■■■■
The gracious front portico is a setting for afternoon luncheons and evening cocktails (left). Its original wooden floor was replaced with tiles sometime after 1935.

The town of Greenville, a small pocket of genteel civilization in central Alabama, is dotted with historic homes and public buildings. The downtown district shows the familiar signs of neglect typical in many smaller American cities. But just a few blocks off the main street a Greek Revival cottage sits relatively unscathed by the ravages of time. Six Doric columns stretch neatly across the facade, which is tucked beneath the shade of a large, sprawling magnolia tree. A brass plaque to the left of the front door indicates the house's historical landmark status. What the marker doesn't begin to detail is the prominent role this house has had for over 150 years in the lives of two of the

171

town's founding families.

Butler County, of which Greenville is the county seat, was officially formed in 1819—the same year that Alabama was admitted into the Union. The county is named for Captain William Butler, one of its first settlers. A man of heroic renown, Butler died fending off an Indian attack on March 20, 1818. Still untamed back country up until then, the area was part of the Creek Indian Nation. It's gently undulating hills were populated with thick forests of oak, hickory, pine, chestnut, poplar, and sweet and sour gum trees. These fertile forests and lush ranges were inhabited by large populations of deer, wild turkey, and other species of game birds. The area was undoubtably an Eden of promise to ambitious pioneers who may have felt spurned by the aristocrats of the southern coastal regions. They

braved the wild countryside in exchange for the chance to prosper in Butler County's abundance.

Settlers were once again attracted to the Butler County area in 1819 because the Indian presence was dwindling. This second wave of pioneers included John, James, and Joseph Dunklin of South Carolina. It was typical for family groups to move en masse from an older seaboard state to a frontier district. The well-stocked caravan wandered into a grassy clearing inhabited by wild deer on the evening of January 14, 1819. After scouting nearby areas, they had decided by the following morning to make the pleasant locale their final destination.

Though creature comforts for these early settlers were few and their housing crude, records show their existence in this new settlement was fairly untroubled. Food was plentiful and

the soil fertile. In 1822 the community was named Greenville in memory of the South Carolina district many of the pioneers had left behind in their emigration to the frontier state. Except for the construction of a church and hotel, the township remained relatively undeveloped until the Mobile and Montgomery Railroad arrived just prior to the Civil War, opening up the landlocked settlement to outside influences.

The railroad brought an influx of residents as well as carpenters and bricklayers into the city's population. These craftsmen busily set about constructing the town's first notable homes. Though all of Greenville's early records were destroyed when the county Court House burned, accounts indicate that around 1822, county pioneer Major James Dunklin commissioned some of Greenville's newly arrived skilled laborers to

■■■■■■■■■■■■■■
A reproduction Italian dining table seats ten (far left). An oriental screen hangs behind the buffet. Curtained windows frame what was once a screened porch that was converted into an enclosed sun room during the early 1900s.

■■■■■■■■■■■■■■
The music room is located between the living, dining, and sun room (center).

Wall sconces on either side of the fireplace are Italian antiques, as is the porcelain vase sitting on the mantel.

■■■■■■■■■■■■■■
A double doorway leading from the music room into the front living room frames a view of antique fringed silk damask curtains originally hung in the house during the late 1930s (above).

173

The large gilt mirror sitting just inside the front door is decorated every week with a new bouquet of fresh flowers arranged by a family member (above).

The original parlor was opened up in the mid-1900s into a more livable space (right). Family heirlooms, comfortable overstuffed chairs, and a sofa give the room an easy elegance. A portrait of Frances Beeland Frakes hangs above the mantel.

construct his Herbert Street residence.

Greek Revival was the architectural style in vogue during the time Dunklin built his home. According to *Architecture of the Old South*, James Stuart and Nicholas Revett initiated the trend with their *Antiquities of Athens* publications, which contained illustrations of monuments such as the Temple of Illissus and the Tower of Winds. Greek architectural details began appearing in American books published in Philadelphia around 1818. Settlers brought the popular style with them into Alabama as they moved west from coastal settlements such as Savannah. The popularity of the Greek Revival style was so widespread between 1830 and 1860 that it became known as the National Style.

Though now over 150 years old, the Dunklin house has only changed hands three times since it was first built. Major Dunklin sold the home to a family who inhabited it only one year before it was sold in 1905 to Robert Beeland, a successful Greenville banker and merchant. He established the beginnings of a thriving family community soon to be known as "Beeland Block."

176

Beeland hailed from one of Butler County's later pioneering families. His father, Jefferson, had come to Greenville from Georgia around 1883 and married Leah Frances Thomas, a young woman from one of the town's affluent families. Both survived the perils of the Civil War, but were forced to suffer through its aftermath as the crippled southern economy ruined their comfortable life-style.

The Beeland family's financial security was revived after Jefferson and his oldest son, James, opened the J. Beeland & Son wagon and harness shop, which eventually became the largest

■■■■■■■■■■■■■■
The front guest room's contemporary 1950s twin four-poster beds and curve-shaped side chairs show how Frances liberally mixes furnishing styles (above left).

■■■■■■■■■■■■■■
A grouping of Royal Copenhagen bone porcelain geese decorate a drop-leaf table sitting inside the entry just outside the front bedroom (above right). The Arthur Stewart portrait is of Prather Beeland Nielsen.

■■■■■■■■■■■■■
An epergne filled with fresh roses was a wedding present from a relative of the original homeowners to a Beeland ancestor (left). The table is set for ten with Wedgwood bone china, pearl-handled knives, and Towle sterling forks and spoons. Frances bought the antique serving dishes and the pair of candelabra in London.

■■■■■■■■■■■■■
Oriental accents dominate the living room's interior, as seen in this detail shot of the wallpaper and vase displayed on the fireplace mantel (above).

■■■■■■■■■■■■■
Above the fireplace, Arthur Stewart's portrait of Connie Beeland Nielsen faces out across the dining room. The walls are adorned with a muted red and green oriental-patterned paper (right).

department store between Montgomery and Mobile. Robert, the third Beeland son, used his family's growing fortunes to build a legacy for his heirs. He founded the First National Bank of Greenville, operated five cotton gins, and donated the land for the town's main park. He provided an exclusive life-style for his children and grandchildren, who lived within a two-block area. Fresh milk and butter from his private dairy as well as vegetables from his farm were delivered each morning to all of the family doorsteps.

Quality comforts were certainly priorities for the family. So it is not surprising that installing indoor plumbing was Robert's first contribution to the Herbert Street house. He took another step in upgrading the modern accommodations by converting a back bedroom into a kitchen. The kitchen was originally located in a separate structure behind the house. Kitchens were often built away from the living quarters in early houses to prevent cooking fires from overheating bedrooms and public spaces during the summer. A screened porch off the music room was enclosed and converted into a sun-room with casement windows. These changes provided the house with four bedrooms and three full bathrooms.

No other structural changes were made until Robert's son, Claude, bought the house from his father's estate in 1935 and moved in with his wife, Sara Lou, and their four daughters, Connie, Frances, Joanne, and Prather. Claude enclosed and converted a porch stretching across the back of the house into a den, tiled the wooden front porch, and knocked out a wall and doorway in the entry hall to open up the enclosed front sitting room.

The house is now inhabited by a third Beeland generation. Claude's second daughter, Frances, and her husband, James Frakes, moved into her childhood home in the 1970s so she could be near her three sisters, all of whom live nearby with their families. The Frakeses have made few changes in the house's basic design. They redecorated the kitchen and adjoining breakfast room. An informal great room with French doors was added on the back of the right wing. The new space was built as an office and art studio, where Frances paints and creates needlepoint designs she is commissioned to do. A wooden stairway leads down into a covered two-car parking area.

Original rooms in the house are Alabama heart of pine. The home's original wide-plank pine floor lay protected and unseen beneath narrow oak floorboards. The Dunklins had had the second layer of flooring laid down to hide the then-unfashionable pine boards.

Identically matching exterior and interior trim moldings are the most distinctive architectural features. Flat, block-patterned dental moldings run along decorative crowns above front exterior windows and are repeated above inside windows and on a larger scale over double doorways leading into the living, dining, and music rooms and a front bedroom.

The house still has its original front door; its sturdy peg construction has withstood constant use and is still framed above and on the sides by the original lead glass windowpanes. The living room is furnished with a mixture of deeply cushioned upholstered pieces and inherited antiques, such as a gilt mirror and side table. Each week the mirror serves as a backdrop for an elaborate fresh floral arrangement. The air of southern gentility that stirs about the house is captured in this floral tradition,

■■■■■■■■■■■■■■■■
French doors from the
music room and formal
dining room open into
the sun-room, which
is furnished with a
comfortable sofa and
chairs (left).

■■■■■■■■■■■■■■■■
Shutters covering the
windows in the small side
room keep the midday
Alabama heat out and
filter in just enough
daylight (below).

which Frances learned from her mother.

A double doorway leads into the music room, where a baby grand piano fills a corner. Bookshelves line the back of the hallway wall and are filled with art and travel books, family photographs, and memorabilia collected during the couple's trips through distant lands. Rosewood love seats and a mother-of-pearl inlaid papier-mâché table originally bought for the living room by the last Mrs. Beeland are mixed with Italian antiques.

French doors open off this space onto a casual sun room. A third seating arrangement of several cozy upholstered chairs and a sofa fill the small area, which makes a quiet retreat for reading or writing. The music room also opens onto the formal dining room, where ten chairs are pulled around the expansive Italian reproduction table. An elegant wallpaper patterned

with an oriental design establishes the tone of this room's decor, which is accented by an antique oriental screen hung above the buffet. Antique sterling serving dishes, bone china, and pearl-handled flatware add delicate touches to the dramatic decor.

All of the house's front rooms radiate southern hospitality and charm. The furnishings' timeless designs are neither very formal nor casual, but are instead a mixture of graceful ease that reflects the Frakeses' life-style. Being with family and friends is their first priority, and the rooms in their house reflect this tradition. The couple graciously welcomes lifelong friends and first-time acquaintances into their home.

Each year the spirit of their extended family fills the house on Christmas evening. Three generations of Robert Beeland's descendants, including eighteen of his great-great-grandchildren, gather in the house to sing, dance, and enjoy the holiday together.

This annual celebration is just one of many occasions during the year when the four sisters' families gather in the house. They celebrate their mutual friendships with afternoon cocktails, frequent dinner parties, and family vacations. Their conversations are peppered with fond memories of life within Beeland Block. As their lives change through the passing of time, the Herbert Street house remains a familiar constant. Its facade remains unchanged and it stands as it always has, open and welcoming, what Frances Beeland Frakes calls the family "anchor" for generations to come.

■■■■■■■■■■■■■■■■
Just after buying the house from his father's estate, Claude Beeland converted the former screen porch into a more protected environment. His father, Robert, originally bought the wicker furniture for the sun room in the 1900s (left).

■■■■■■■■■■■■■■■■
A breakfast room with built-in cabinets and shelves connects the dining room to the kitchen (above).

■■■■■■■■■■■■■■■■
The perfume of magnolia blossoms scents the summer evening air with a seductive fragrance (right).

The mirrored dresser and the bed are part of a bedroom set given to Leah and Jefferson Beeland, the family's matriarch and patriarch, as a wedding present around 1860 (left). Their four sons and two daughters were all born in this bed, as were many other Beelands.

Delicate trim work on a heirloom linen contributes to the guest room's feminine feeling (above).

The family heirloom bed is made up with antique linens and throw pillows with crocheted covers (right). The colorful quilt is a family heirloom sewn by Frakes's grandmother and is reputed to have won a prize at the Kentucky state fair.

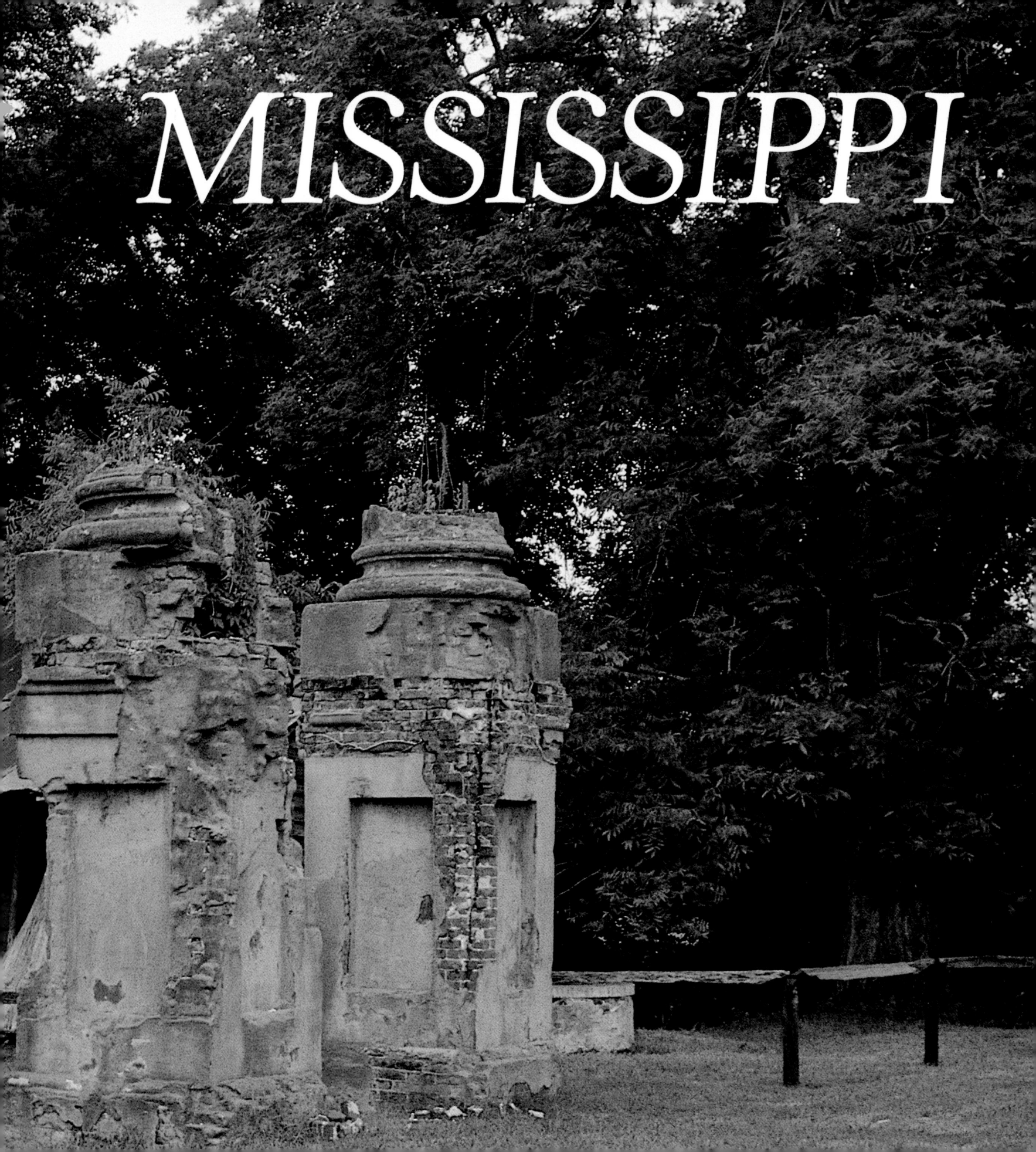

MISSISSIPPI

Flowerree Estate

A MISSISSIPPI ITALIANATE MANSION

Vicksburg is built on a series of staggered bluffs above the ambling curves of the Mississippi River between New Orleans and Memphis. This sleepy town is most often remembered as the site of one of the Civil War's important fights, one fought and lost by the Confederate army in 1863. But Vicksburg's historical significance extends beyond the battlefield: Not only did Joseph Biedenharn bottle the first Coca-Cola here in 1894, but the city's streets are lined with lovely mansions reflecting the town's diverse design history.

The French were the first to inhabit the area surrounding Vicksburg when they bought land from the Indians in 1680 and established a trad-

A row of nineteenth century English Queen Anne chairs, early antique purchases made by the homeowners, make an interesting entry hall composition (left). The nineteenth century oil portait of an anonymous Englishwoman hangs over an American Sheraton card table of the same period.

The outline of the original portico's twenty-two wooden columns was duplicated and replaced by more permanent masonry pillars (above). Smooth bricks imported from England were used for the facade. Handsome brackets were paired across the front of the two-and-a-half-story house above the first and second floors' segmentally arched windows.

A seating arrangement of wrought-iron garden chairs from the Birmingham Ironworks overlooks the backyard lap (left).

The three-room servant house off to the right side of the house was already built on the property when Colonel Flowerree purchased the land in the early 1870s (above).

ing center at Fort St. Pierre. The Spanish arrived in 1790 and established their own fortification Fort Nogales (*nogales* is the Spanish word for "walnut" and refers to the variety of trees growing abundantly along the river bluffs). The actual town wasn't established until Reverend Newitt Vick, a circuit-riding Methodist minister from Virginia, arrived in 1812 and bought land nearby and founded a mission. Vick died before the town was completely laid out, but the executor of his will completed the task and named it after him. The city was incorporated on January 29, 1825.

A flourishing trade port quickly developed for the loading and shipping of cotton grown on the large area plantations. Flush with commerce, the city attracted a colorful lot of characters, such as gamblers, who helped shape the city's then-notorious reputation as a gaming center. Vicksburg expanded to a river port with 2,500 inhabitants by 1835, and life went on as usual until the city became a battleground.

The struggle between the Union and Confederate forces began with a gunboat bombardment in 1862. A campaign of destruction waged by Union generals demolished surrounding areas and developed into a land and water siege on Vicksburg in 1863 that lasted for forty-seven days. Citizens crowded into clay caves for protection from the thundering crash of cannon and many lost homes and businesses. The bombardments ended when Confederate General John C. Pemberton surrendered to General Grant on July 4. The memory of the loss still remains strong with Vicksburg residents. Though the victory was the Union's most expensive war trophy, in terms of the number of men lost and time involved, it was a turning point in the war that brought on the imminent demise of the Confederate army.

At the war's end, the city's damaged landscape was gradually revived as the riverport's economy rebounded. Mansions with picturesque names such as Cedar Grove and McRaven replaced war-torn buildings. Today, the gracious homes stand within a forty-square-block historic district. Flowerree, an Italianate treasure perched just above the river behind railroad tracks running along Pearl Street, is the home of Skip Tuminello, a highly respected southern architect.

Tuminello grew up in Vicksburg during the city's waning frontier days. He recalls the showboat days when refurbished towboats routinely navigated the river, dropping anchor so merrymakers could ferry over and board the floating palaces for party-filled evenings.

He remembers the city before any of its buildings were reno-

■■■■■■■■■■■■■■■
An original glass pane over
the house's front door
filters soft daylight across
the heart pine floor and up
onto the walnut and
chestnut staircase (left).

■■■■■■■■■■■■■■■
Blue and red porcelain
inserts decorate the
walnut newel post at the
staircase's first-floor
landing (below).

■■■■■■■■■■■■■■■
An oval arch above the
double parlor's front alcove
is decorated with rococo-
style plaster work crafted
by Bavarian immigrants
(near right).

■■■■■■■■■■■■■■■
A Chippendale love seat
inherited from Skip
Tuminello's mother sits
in front of a full-figure
portrait of Gayle
Tuminello (far right).

vated. He and his boyhood friends spent afternoons exploring waterfront ruins and the crumbling shells of grand Federal, Romanesque, and Greek Revival houses. Yet Tuminello's youthful interest in architecture was keener than simple explorations among abandoned buildings. He built elaborate model houses in his family's rose garden using miniature clay bricks he baked in his mother's oven and discarded wooden spools from his grandmother's sewing basket for columns. Tuminello attributes his early obsession for buildings to the looming presence of Flowerree, just two doors away from his childhood home.

The house was built by Colonel Charles Conway Flowerree, who arrived in Vicksburg shortly after the Civil War in 1866. At this time, Mississippi was facing the impact of its Civil War defeat. Large antebellum plantation mansions around Vicksburg stood gaunt, unpainted, and unkempt. Colonel Flowerree undoubtedly believed the area was his promised land, for after fighting in the battle of Manassas and becoming the Confederate Army's youngest full colonel at age nineteen, the young Virginian made Vicksburg his home. He quickly prospered in the Mississippi port, becoming one of the town's prominent postbellum businessmen and serving as postmaster during President Grover Cleveland's second administration before marrying Jennie Wilson and joining with her father, Victor, in an ice supply business. Shortly thereafter, his own father and brother joined him and the three men formed the successful D. W. Flowerree Ice Company, which supplied block ice to the town's residents.

193

■■■■■■■■■■■■■■■■
The Tuminellos' first
antique purchase was
the circa 1830 walnut
dining table, produced
by Vicksburg craftsmen,
around which nineteenth
century Queen Anne
chairs sit. The American
Empire sideboard was
crafted down the river
in New Orleans (left).

■■■■■■■■■■■■■■■■
The terra-cotta paint used
in the dining room is
identical to the room's
original color. The dining
room's Carrara marble
mantelpiece was bought in
New Orleans (near right).

■■■■■■■■■■■■■■■■
The natural grain of the
cypress molding is exposed
in the library doorway,
where layers of paint were
scraped away (far right).

By the early 1870s, Charles Flowerree decided to enjoy the wealth of his lucrative business pursuits by building a trophy home for himself and his growing family. He paid $3,000 for the property where Flowerree now stands. Though records vaguely describe what structures stood on the lot when the colonel purchased the property, it is known the house was completed in 1872.

Colonel Flowerree obviously spared no expense in the construction of his High Victorian Italianate home. Though the architect or builder's identities remain unknown, this design was much in vogue. According to Virginia and Lee McAlester's *A Field Guide to American Houses*, the first Italianate houses in the United States were built during the 1830s. The style was popularized shortly afterward by pattern books published by

Andrew Jackson Downing in the 1840s. During the 1850s, the style's popularity grew until it became a dominant design used in the construction of both public and private buildings throughout American frontier boomtowns.

The colonel's heirs occupied Flowerree until 1929, when it was sold to state Senator S. J. McCauley, who did the elegant structure a disfavor by converting the home into a boardinghouse and renting it out to railroad workers during the next twenty years. The house was stripped of many valuable ornamental details during this period. Decorative gold and platinum moldings in the drawing room were removed and sold or stolen, as were eight of nine original Carrara marble mantels. What did remain were ornate plaster center roses, ceiling and crown moldings crafted with a rococo period influence by Bavar-

■■■■■■■■■■■■■■
Religious icons purchased
from a convent auction
hang above the master bed.
Scalamandre silk curtains
and a canopy envelop the
king-sized bed. Wooden
columns salvaged from
the original portico were
used to build the tester
bed (left).

■■■■■■■■■■■■■■
The upholstered two-piece
Louis XIV chaise is
eighteenth century. The
large end rug is one of two
Soumacks dating back to
1830 (right).

ian immigrants who settled in the city before the war between the states. Architectural historians still consider these delicate designs as some of the South's finest Italianate art.

The layout of the structure's remaining six thousand original square feet is today much as it was when the colonel moved in. A four-thousand-square-foot *garçonniere* connected by an arcade to the back of the house contained the first floor kitchen, which measured thirteen-by-thirty feet, a two-storey privy and second-floor bedrooms for two of the colonel's three sons. It and several original outbuildings were demolished in 1960 by a young couple who owned the house for a short time. The structure sustained additional damage when a tornado whipped through the town, tearing off the slate roof and destroying all of the chimneys.

By this time, Flowerree was rapidly sinking into a state of total deterioration as rats and pigeons were nesting in the house. Worse still were the water leaks damaging the library and parlor's plaster moldings and creating mud buildup throughout the basement floor. The owners then had neither the finances nor experience to restore the damaged property, so they sold the house to Skip Tuminello, who had yearned to own the house since childhood.

Skip and his wife, Gayle, bought the property in 1961 for a bargain price of $8,000 while he was still attending architectural school. The purchase quickly dictated the couple's personal plans and established the direction of Skip's career. He had long wanted to establish Vicksburg's first architectural practice and planned to build and live in a postmodern house overlooking

■■■■■■■■■■■■■■■■
Southern heirlooms
decorating the house
include an antique globe
lamp that illuminates the
guest room's formal decor.

the river. Purchasing Flowerree eliminated the couple's need for a contemporary home, and Skip's restoration work on the historic structure won him his first architectural position. The experience also helped him knowledgeably approach restoration work on other Vicksburg structures, such as his own office building, which dates back to the eighteenth century, as well as hundreds of showplace homes scattered across the South.

The restoration of Flowerree is a testament to Skip's skill. Replacing Flowerree's roof was Gayle and Skip's initial project. They accomplished the task while commuting between college in New Orleans and Vicksburg on weekends before Skip's graduation. They then moved back to Vicksburg and lived with Skip's parents until Flowerree's earthen basement and dining room were cleaned and renovated into an efficiency apartment, where they lived as they slowly reclaimed additional rooms one at a time. Six months later, after Gayle hand-sanded and scraped thick layers of boxcar-red paint left over from the boardinghouse days off the library's cypress door moldings, their living quarters expanded to three rooms. Beneath the offensive red layers she uncovered a delicate morning glory vine painted across the library's ceiling, and the dining room ceiling's original banana leaf pattern.

With help, the Tuminellos repaired the front portico by replacing weather-damaged clusters of twenty-two wooden columns with masonry pillars. Enough of the original columns were salvaged to serve as support posters for the master room's king-sized bed. The second-floor balcony suspended just above the portico remains the best vantage point from which to watch tugs and boats moving up and down the river.

Entry to the front is gained through a simple wooden door. An etched glass transom original to the house softly filters daylight from over the door onto the hall's heart pine floor and is one of the home's most significant details. The drama of the house's spacious interiors begins just inside the door with a massive, walnut veneer newel post inset with blue and red porcelain patterns. Colonel Flowerree must have desired a distinctive statement for his entry, for this handsome element, though made of wood indigenous to the area, was crafted for the late 1880s Chicago World's Fair and is atypical of others used in Vicksburg houses.

The house is solid brick, except for a library wall dominated by wooden bookshelves. Smooth bricks imported from England were used to build the front facade, but the rest of the structure was built with hand-milled bricks and corbels baked on site in a backyard kiln. This same kiln produced bricks for several other

■■■■■■■■■■■■■■■

Colonel Flowerree's second-floor bedroom overlooking the back courtyard is now used as a guest room. All of the furnishings are American antiques, except the pie crust table, which is eighteenth century English (left).

■■■■■■■■■■■■■■■

A grouping of antique crystal and sterling bottles and jars collected through the years decorates an American Empire desk, circa 1800, in the guest bedroom (right).

grand neighborhood homes. Two-foot-thick walls were built with air spaces between the brick and plaster to allow air circulation to make the house dry in the winter and cool in the summer. Tuminello claims that the home's construction is better than many others he has restored. Comfort, as well as structural quality, was another of the home's important design elements; Flowerree was one of the first houses in the city built with indoor plumbing. The colonel's indoor bathroom was connected to his second-floor bedroom, which now serves as the guest room.

200

Two doorways lead off the entry hall into the parlor. One of only three double parlors in the city, the room is impressive in scale as well as detail. Typically, the oversized room would have been split in the middle with paneled sliding or pocket doors so men and women could congregate in separate areas. The fact that the room is unbroken indicates the Flowerree's entertained on a large scale, making the more traditional setup inadequate. The undivided space also gives the room impressive proportions, for with a fifteen-foot ceiling it is as tall as it is wide and then twice as long.

nally covered in gold leafing. Most of the heavily paneled doors measure ten feet tall by thirty-nine inches wide. Initially, the cypress doorways were painted with a faux rosewood finish, because in the 1870s, fruitwood grains were fashionably acceptable while decorative woods and evergreens were not.

To the right of the entrance hall are two doors leading into the library and dining room. The magnolia-blossom design of the library's plaster chandelier center rose is rare. Though it is the state flower, this particular floral pattern is rarely duplicated in plaster work. Scraping and sanding through layers of old paint revealed that the dark green room was originally painted a flat tan. An open doorway cut into a wall of bookshelves leads into the dining room. Painted the original terra-cotta, this room contains a Carrara marble mantel.

To the right of this is the former butler's pantry, which Tuminello converted into a modern brick-walled kitchen by recycling the former kitchen's cypress wainscoting as storage cabinets. The kitchen's working area opens on to a semioctagonal breakfast room added in 1971 where the privy once stood, with a brick walkway to the *garçonniere*.

Up on the second floor, four massive doors now open onto three instead of the original four bedrooms. To the right of the walnut and chestnut staircase, the guest room connects with the Tuminello's daughter, Dominique's, room. On the left, a partition was removed to give the master bedroom the same dimensions as the parlor. At the back of this room, a square, columned gallery which ran the length of the parlor and entrance hall and overlooked the back courtyard was enclosed and converted into a bathroom and dressing room area. Though each bedroom has a fireplace, the decorative details are significantly more conservative than the elaborate ones found in the first floor's public rooms.

A third-floor attic space was converted into a bedroom suite for the Tuminellos' two sons, Steven and John. The open space is simply finished and furnished with beds and worktables.

The house is furnished with an impressive collection of antiques that includes Louis XIV as well as American Empire pieces. The couple first purchased antiques at Vicksburg estate auctions while still in college because, though older furnishings were not in vogue, they were extremely inexpensive. The Tuminellos' early antique investments paid off when they moved into Flowerree, since the home's grand scale is the ideal setting for the large, wooden wardrobes, beds, and chests. The only element missing from the completely restored home is a view of a showboat dropping anchor on the riverfront below.

Though the room contains turn-of-the-century crystal chandeliers, priceless Italian portraits, Chippendale love seats, and an 1810 Steinway piano, the viewer's eye is drawn to a single graceful archway leading into a shuttered bay window alcove. Ruined by decades of water damage, the flattened arch is now gloriously restored with an intricate ornamental texture of finely crafted scrolls and buttons.

All of the cypress doors hanging throughout the house are original to its construction. Each one is fitted with original nine-by-nine bronze door hinges dating back to 1860 that were origi-

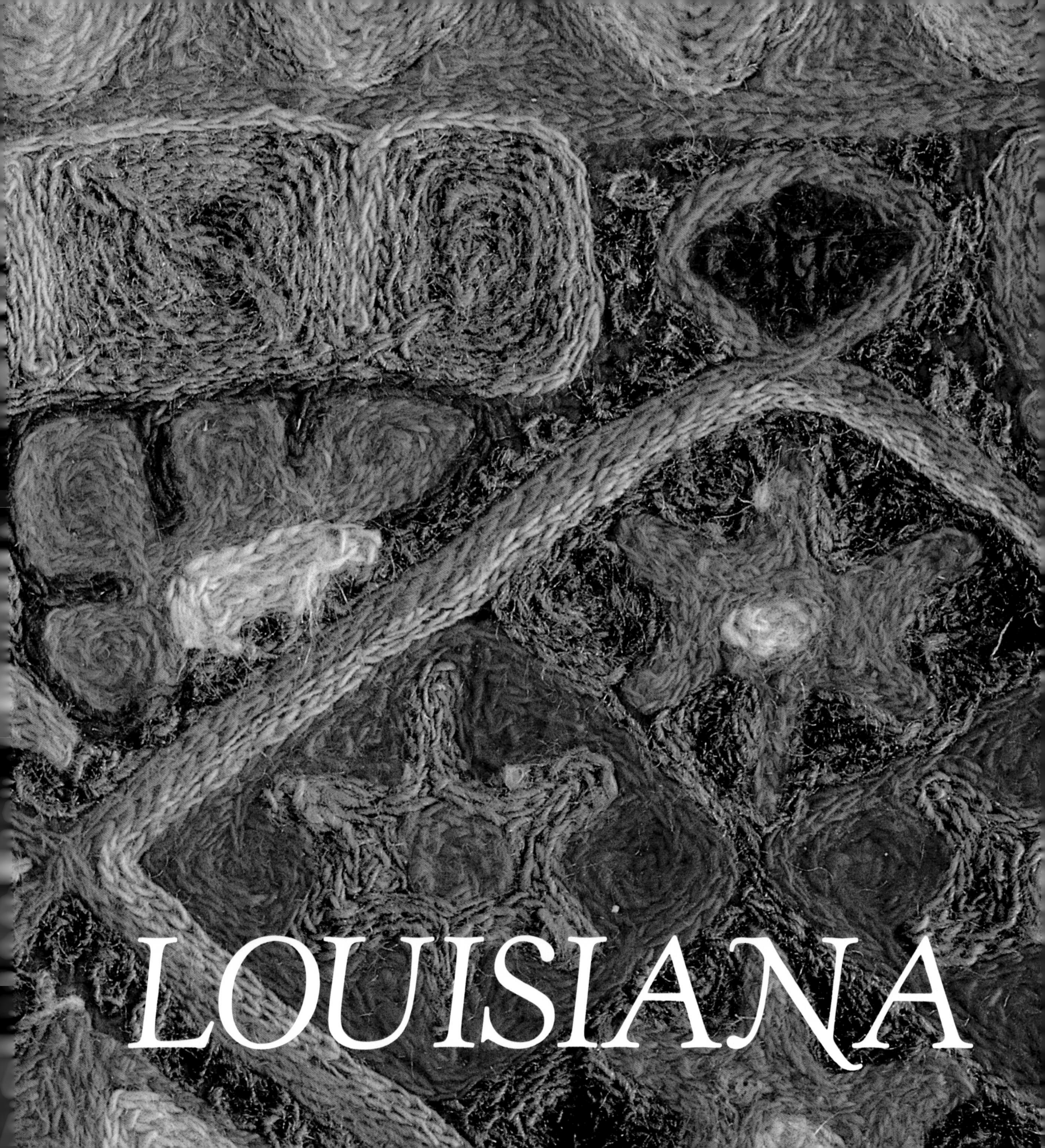

LOUISIANA

IN THE ETERNAL FRUIT TREE YOUR
FRUITS GIVE OFF THEIR AROMAS
YOUR FLOWERS GIVE THEIR COLOR
GROWING WITH THE JOY OF THE
WINDS AND THE BLOSSOMS. DO NOT
STOP GIVING THIRST TO THE
TREE THAT TREASURED YOUR
SEED "DIEGO" IS THE NAME
OF LOVE. TE AMO DIEGO. FRIDA.

Uptown Artistry

CREATIVE LIVING IN LOUISIANA

A s New Orleans' St. Charles Avenue streetcar line meanders away from the the city's Garden District, it passes by lush parks before entering a grid of landscaped streets in the residential area once known as Jefferson City and now known as Uptown. Laid out on a former plantation site, the neighborhood is now home to both Tulane and Loyola universities as well as parks, fine restaurants, antique shops, boutiques, and beautifully restored homes. Examples of Greek Revival, Italianate, Queen Anne, Tudor, and Renaissance architecture grace the handsome thoroughfares. One of the neighborhood's more distinctive side streets is Marengo Street, for it bears the local

■■■■■■■■■■■■■■■

The entry foyer sideboard was a bargain find. Two juju dolls made by New Orleans artist Lois Simbach are displayed alongside dancing bears by artist Robert Hutchinson and an angel by Louisiana folk artist Louise Gendron (left).

■■■■■■■■■■■■■■■

The two-story pink and teal Colonial Revival built in 1895 is located on Uptown, New Orleans's Marengo Street, locally known as "Artists Row" (above). The house's decorative plaster and wood swags running beneath the first- and second-story overhangs are detailed with garlands and ribbons.

205

The 1930s entry hall's slim stained-glass windows were bought as replacements for the vandalized originals. The *retables* and snake displayed on the sideboard are by Enidina (above).

An heirloom Louis XVI recamier in the front entry sits before the grand staircase landing. Beneath the staircase hangs one of Sandra Blair-Richardson's recent paintings (right).

■■■■■■■■■■■■■■
The home's thematic decor begins just inside the front door with the front living room's dramatic African collection. Luis Colmenares' custom brass and steel coffee table frame is topped by Nanci Roark's sandblasted glass. An etching by New Orleans architect Gary Brandom hangs above the fireplace. The room's art mix is personalized by an acrylic resin female torso made by Robert and a large ceramic bowl displayed on the coffee table made by Sandra. The Hertiz rug covering the floor is a red color typical to southern interiors (below, center, and far right).

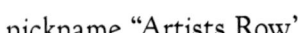

nickname "Artists Row."

Painters, sculptors, art professors, and museum directors are among those who reside on Marengo Street. That the city's art community has adopted this broad Uptown thoroughfare as its premier address is significant because New Orleans is a hotbed of cultural influences ranging from the decorative to the culinary. Sandra Blair-Richardson, local artist, gallery owner, and crafts director for the internationally acclaimed New Orleans Jazz and Heritage Festival, is a Marengo Street resident whose home and art are testaments to the city's creative energies. Located a few blocks off St. Charles, the Colonial Revival exterior reverberates a cheerful energy beneath coats of pink and teal. Inside, rooms are filled with a mad mix of graceful antiques and contemporary crafts.

A native of Milwaukee, Richardson adopted New Orleans after a job transfer brought her to the city in the early 1970s. Though she had little formal art training, she quickly broke into local fame by staging a Mardi Gras parade mocking the city's aristocracy, calling them the "Krewe of Clones."

Next, she became crafts director for the city's Jazz Fest, considered to be the world's largest music festival. The directorship brought her in contact with craftspersons and artists inside and outside Louisiana and led her to found the nonprofit Rhino Gallery in New Orleans' central business district and to recently open the Warehouse District's Chihauhau Gallery.

Uptown, where Richardson lives, is a suburb of New Orleans that sprawls along the east bank of the Mississippi River. The district became the favored address for the influx of Americans

coming into the city after the Louisiana Purchase in 1803. Though born out of an agrarian society, Uptown, then called Jefferson City, matured between 1870 and 1910 when New Orleans' population boomed. Jefferson's transformation into a suburb was aided by the arrival of trolly lines, seven of which were in place as early as 1881. The district's look was also shaped by a developing demand among newly affluent families for large, fashionable residences.

Albert Toledano and Ferdinand Reusch, Jr., of the firm Toledano & Reusch were two architects actively working in the district. They are the architects of record for the Richardson's Marengo Street house, having designed and built the two-story frame structure in 1895 for a total of $6,000.

Variations of the Colonial Revival style are common along Uptown streets. The Richardson house is a whimsical interpretation of the style, with its detailed plaster and wood swags decorated with garlands and ribbons hanging along the first and second stories. After they married in 1984, Robert and Sandra Richardson bought the house from an elderly couple who had operated it as a boardinghouse. Though Sandra was discouraged by the house's dark, neglected state, Robert saw its potential and convinced his wife that with work it would make a good home.

The house is built a few feet above ground, as most New Orleans buildings are, to guard against wood rot brought on by the city's humid climate. The Richardsons' initial tasks were replacing the rotted roof and painting the exterior. Sandra selected the paint colors for the outside in the same manner she

A dining room vignette is topped by Charlie Miner's Tiffany-style dish. Stacks of the family's formal dinnerware crafted by Charlie Bohn share space with artist Barbara Threefeet's humorous ceramic feet (above).

The dining room is a harmonious mixture of new and old. Tom Ladousa's flying chicken sculpture and a Clifton Webb totem are humorous accents to the Louis XVI table and chairs. The eighteen-foot Chinese-weave rug is a rare Nicholls deco piece crafted in the 1920s (right).

211

approaches art projects. She sketched the structure, had it copied, and then, using colored pencils, colored each copy in different combinations, such as peach with lavender trim and green with purple. The house's existing shades of pink and teal were selected by family vote.

Interior modifications included the removal of linoleum tiles from the structure's original pine floors and several interior walls to create larger rooms. The most extensive do-it-yourself family project was the addition of a sun room. Sandra and Robert spent three months sledgehammering through an exterior wall on evenings and weekends to accommodate the addition.

The downstairs interiors are a charming, impromptu mix of antiques, arts, and crafts. Each room reverberates with a singular personality that closely reflects Sandra's ongoing artistic ex-

ploits and interests. She gives herself a great deal of decorative freedom because she views her house as a "playground." This lighthearted approach lets her add to and alter a room as her personal tastes evolve and change. Her fascination with southwestern style is echoed in the kitchen's decor, where she is transforming an Italian country decor into a Santa Fe motif. In the sitting room, when she developed a dislike for a floral wallpaper pattern, she salvaged it with a session of sponge painting.

Sandra's working relationships with other artists enrich the collection of arts and crafts displayed throughout the house. Her criterion for buying art is that each work must be by an artist she knows and likes. This rule enriches and animates the family collection because there is a story attached to every item, whether it is a hand-blown glass dish, a painting, or a sculpture.

212

Sandra has tackled the task of organizing the ever-expanding collection by theming and decorating each of the six downstairs rooms as a separate showcase. Visitors are introduced to this approach just inside the front door, where the entry sideboard displays a vignette of Sandra's favorite collections—religious icons. A *santos*, juju dolls, and two traditional Mexican altar scenes known as *retables* are clustered together.

The religious theme extends into the living room, where an African art collection begun by Robert is exhibited. The dark, primitive beauty of the African pieces, most of which are of Mali origin, is highlighted against rose-toned walls. The Richardsons prize this collection because each item was designed to fill a functional, everyday purpose, whether it was of a religious or household nature.

The Richardsons' collection also contains items that beautify as well as compliment their life-style. They dine exclusively off handmade pottery each evening, and rooms on both the first and second floors are illuminated by streams of colored sunlight filtered in through stained-glass windows purchased as replacements for now-vandalized or stolen original panes. The oldest stained-glass windows in the house, which date back to 1890, hang in the sun room. Panes installed in the bottom of three kitchen windows were crafted by New Orleans artist Joy Schroeder in a pattern that mimics the design of late nineteenth century transom windows. The entry hall's slim blue and gold windows date back to the 1930s and were removed from an Ohio estate. The black and white marble bath off the second-floor master bedroom is illuminated by a pair of hundred-year-

■■■■■■■■■■■■■■■■■

The plain lines of this corner kitchen chair are transformed into an eye-catching prop by hieroglypic designs and colorful patterns by Perry Morgan (left).

■■■■■■■■■■■■■■■■■

A good-luck lizard inspired by Santa Fe folklore belly-crawls across Sandra's kinetically patterned floor cloth (below).

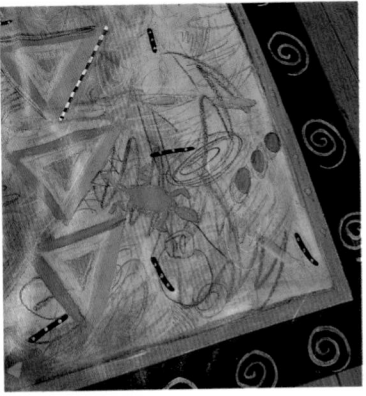

■■■■■■■■■■■■■■■■■

Robert Richardson's geometric shapes explode off the kitchen walls and counters and punctuate the room's decorative mix of Italian country and southwestern influences (right). The red-oak cabinets were custom-built for the room. Joy Schroeder's stained-glass panes provide privacy while allowing light to filter into the spacious room.

old church windows.

The layout of the front public rooms follows the original floor plan. The front door opens into a foyer that contains the front, formal staircase. Large open doorways lead into the living room on the right and straight back into a dining room. Turn-of-the-century lace curtains hung across the living and dining room windows provide privacy and allow soft daylight to stream in.

Some of Sandra's biggest decorative risks to date were taken in a smaller sitting room the family named the "Retreat." Originally designed as one-half of the double parlor, the room is set up as a separate area. Sandra initially papered the room with a country floral design. She disliked the paper's delicate look after

it was hung, but instead of removing it she sponge-painted over the pattern and achieved a muted effect. This room also contains the house's boldest furniture creation. Relying on her artistic flair again, Sandra converted her youngest child's brass baby bed into a canopied settee and made it the central focus of a seating area.

A dramatic combination of influences dominates the dining room, where the family sits down each evening at a Louis XVI table to dine by candlelight off handmade pottery dinnerware with utensils embellished with art paper on the handles. The table and chairs are Richardson family heirlooms. The tablecloth is an Egyptian folk rug crafted by children, and the art-

work filling the room includes a flying chicken, hand-blown art glass, antique French oil paintings, and a pair of ceramic feet.

In the kitchen, the original Italian country theme has taken a more recent detour in a southwestern direction. Custom red-oak cabinets hint at the room's former theme. The now-muted peach walls are framed by pepper-green moldings. Colorful floor cloths and wooden stools painted by Sandra with kinetic designs and shapes bracket the bold black-and-white tiled countertops. An angel and shell-covered cross nailed above the sink is framed by generous bouquets of chili ristras.

A kitchen highlight is the lizard tile border created by artist Maggie Towne. The multicolored figures placed head to head and head to tail are inset between the backsplash tiles. Sandra commissioned the lizard design because the reptiles are a symbol for good luck in Santa Fe, New Mexico, one of her favorite haunts.

A back set of stairs hidden behind a side door leads up into a second-floor sitting area. The new sun room connected to the left of the kitchen by open doorways is where the Richardsons gather for evening club soda cocktails with their children. The

216

window-filled room looks out over a small landscaped yard decorated with colorful PVC pipe sculptures by New Orleans artist Dexter Stewart.

The upstairs sleeping quarters are the next area targeted for interior alteration. Sandra jokingly says her family lives in fear of what decorative attack plans she has for their bedrooms. But really there is little she could do to surprise them or any other New Orleans locals, for as Sandra concludes, "This city is based around a party theme, which is why my house doesn't shock anyone living here."

■■■■■■■■■■■■■■■
The hundred-year-old church window lends a serene air to the second-floor black and white marble-tiled master bath. The wall behind the basin is adorned by Sandra's painted vine border (above).

ARKANSAS

Craftsman Classic

ARCHITECTURAL HISTORY IN ARKANSAS

Built in 1917, the Craftsman-style house stands on a corner in Little Rock's historic Quapaw Quarter (above).

A local artisan copied the shield pattern in a window installed in the home's front door during the 1934 renovation to create a reproduction pane authentic in size to the door's original design (left).

The Arkansas River gently winds through the region that was once the old Louisiana Purchase. It passes the eastern foothills of the Ouachita Mountains on its journey to join the "Big Muddy." The Arkansas River, the second largest tributary of the Mississippi, served as a traveler's highway when the first inhabitants journeyed to the area now recognized as Little Rock. The first residents, the Quapaw Indians, arrived in the early seventeenth century. They landed at an outcrop of stones they named "Point of Rocks" after traveling from Kentucky down the Mississippi River and then into the Arkansas River Valley. The Indians established a number of small villages several generations

221

prior to the arrival of the first white settler.

Frenchman Bernard de la Harpe was the first white explorer to lay eyes on the "Point of Rocks" in 1722. Scottish financier John Law, who held the title "Duke of Arkansas," had received eighty-two thousand acres of land in the territorial wilderness. He employed de la Harpe as a lieutenant and sent him to gather information about the various Indian tribes living in the area. At the time of de la Harpe's arrival, the Indians were calling a segment of the area the "Green Rock." This nickname gave the explorer the grand expectation of discovering a giant emerald

222

■■■■■■■■■■■■■■■

The entry's eight oak-finished plaster brackets mounted in the entry doorways are reproductions of originals found in an English pub (above).

■■■■■■■■■■■■■■■

An antique mahogany pedestal table, originally used in a Mississippi plantation home, dominates the entry view across into the dining room passageway and the front living room (above).

along the river. Instead, what he found was nothing more than an oversized, common rock coated in green moss. He christened the smaller outcrop of stones downstream on the river's south bank "La Petite Roche," or the Little Rock. "Little Rock" became the starting point for all early surveys of the city, and later on, when the the town was established, the area around the rock became the landing point for commercial river vessels.

In 1818 the Indians signed a treaty relinquishing their claim to certain lands beyond the boundaries of the Quapaw Indian nation. The western edge of their area was established on what

became known as the Quapaw Line, which ran from the Saline River to the Little Rock landmark. The following year the first white settlers arrived from Missouri and founded Little Rock as a centrally located town that would become the capital of the new Territory of Arkansas.

The Quapaw Line existed as the boundary between the city and the Indian nation until 1824, when the Quapaws ceded all their remaining lands in Arkansas over to the U. S. government. Though defunct as an actual division between the two civilizations, the line was still an invisible boundary between

Little Rock and its suburbs as the metropolitan area grew westward. The city's most desirable "old" residential area developed within the parameter of this area as the population grew and people prospered. The original inhabitants were honored in 1961 when the area's historic preservation and restoration district was created and given the name Quapaw Quarter.

At the zenith of its stylish days, the Quapaw Quarter attracted ambitious people such as Ed Cornish from a rural area of the state. Cornish was a real estate and banking tycoon who accumulated great influence and wealth in Little Rock at the turn of the century. He also enjoyed a high profile as the first person to own and drive a Rolls Royce in the state of Arkansas. When he was forty-six, he built a landmark house that suited his reputation. Cornish commissioned a local architect, Theo Sanders, to build a contemporary residence in the fashionable Quapaw Quarter.

Sanders was also a man whose reputation preceded him. The Little Rock native studied architecture in Paris before returning to his hometown to embark on an illustrious design career that included a partnership with Frank Ginocchio and Charles Thompson, the most prolific Arkansas architect of his age. The Cornish house stands as one of Sanders's grand achievements.

The spectacular house represents a combination of the most fashionable building trends of the early twentieth century. Cornish assigned Sanders the task of studying San Francisco and New York's architectural styles. The home is designed in the Craftsman style. The arts and crafts movement, which originated from 1905 to the early 1920s in southern California, stressed honest, functional design and "craftsmanship." The movement was a reaction against the machine-made, mass-produced, and inordinately ornamental buildings that appeared across the United States during the late nineteenth century. Sanders combined an array of different "natural" materials in an overlay of textures to construct the house. Richly crafted layers of decorative-art detailing juxtaposed against warm rich woodworks, stone, stucco, brick, and tile give the house a characteristic Craftsman design.

The home was fitted with a wealth of modern conveniences, including a vacuum system with brass fittings for hoses built into the baseboards in upstairs and downstairs rooms and along the hallways. On the second floor, each bedroom opened onto its own bathroom.

All the careful planning and thought that went into the design could not protect the structure from neglect and vandalism after the Cornishes sold it in 1933. During this time, affluent

■■■■■■■■■■■■■■■
The richness of Cuban mahogany moldings and beams fills the living room (left). The doors opening into the room from the entry are mahogany on one side and oak on the other to correspond with each room's finish. A rare Archibald Knox—an acclaimed art deco English craftsman—pewter tea service ornaments the coffee table.

■■■■■■■■■■■■■■■
An eighteenth century Venetian mirror hangs above a massive nineteenth century reproduction chest in the living room (above). A bronzed pewter mantel clock decorates the antique.

225

The sun room off the dining room, once furnished by the original owners with wicker chairs, rockers, and tables, is now decorated as a comfortable, sunny retreat with an overstuffed couch and chairs (left).

Four stained-glass windows the owners bought from a local church decorate the first-floor library (above).

The front room, originally designed as a music room, was converted into a library by the owners from the original architect's 1916 plans (right). A nineteenth century leather-topped, nine drawer partner's desk dominates the room.

Little Rock residents abandoned the once popular Quapaw Quarter for more suburban settings.

The house was converted into a nursing home in the 1940s; it operated until 1973. The house was in complete disrepair when preservationists Hampton and Nancy Roy stepped in to restore it in 1978. Its entrances and windows had been boarded over, two-thirds of the windowpanes were missing, all of the doorknobs and light fixtures had been stolen, and much of the electrical wiring and plumbing had been stripped out of the walls by vandals.

The couple had already restored twenty-five structures in and around the city when they found the three-story residence. They had become familiar with the Cornish house when Hampton was directing a nomination of 141 structures designed by Little Rock architect Charles Thompson and his associates – of which Theo Sanders was one – to the National Register of Historic Places. The Cornish house not only was placed on the National Register, but it also gained new owners in the Roys.

Restoring the house was a challenge some felt the Roys were not capable of meeting. "We had a commercial developer who approached us to buy the house within six months of our purchase," remembers Hampton. "He wanted to tear the house

An art deco stencil borders the dining room. The owners stained a Gothic-style chandelier to match the room's mahogany trim (far left).

■■■■■■■■■■■■■■■
A lace tablecloth is a delicate backdrop for heirloom Echt Weimar Kobalt china place settings and family sterling (center).

■■■■■■■■■■■■■■■
A tray filled with heirloom stemware punctuates the dining room with vivid color (below).

down and use the block because he thought it was impossible for us to redo it." Not only had the house been virtually stripped bare of many cosmetic finishes, but extensive work was required to replace all the working systems.

The couple first renovated an outbuilding adjacent to the main house that had previously served as servants' quarters. They lived in these temporary living quarters for the duration of the three-year renovation period.

Working from the Roys' specifications, contractor Jack Young restored the house's first-floor rooms to the original 1916 drawings and plans. The couple changed the design slightly by converting the music room to the right of the front door into a library. Shelving originally intended for the living room, but never installed, was added to the library's design. The Roys

adopted the details from the original floor plans and placed bookcases along four walls. The entry's oak paneling and columns and the interior rooms' mahogany woodwork and paneling were restored after coats of garish Day-Glo pink and green were stripped from the woodwork and walls.

Hampton Roy collaborated with historic architectural graphic artists Becky Witsell and Suzanne Kittrell of Little Rock's Designed Communications firm to duplicate original stencil work found in six rooms. The stencil-work borders had been added to the rooms in 1919 by Steve Cole. Cole was later hired in 1934 by the home's second owner, John Craig, to freshen the decorative detail, during which time the original designs were altered.

Witsell and Kitrell stripped back existing layers of paint, un-

The set of leaded-glass windows were copied from the originals. The original architect centered them above the house's front porch, installing four windows in this room and the fifth in an adjoining bedroom. The walnut bed is Austrian.

covered patches of nearly obliterated detailing, and copied those designs. The artists also had the unusual advantage of working with John Cole, one of Steve's sons, who served as an adviser on the project. He told them what patterns he and his brothers had helped their father apply during the first and second paintings.

The original trim designs are unique because they were created with custom-cut stencils instead of the precut patterns sold through paint stores that were popular during that day. An art deco design edges the dining room's walls. The living room's asymmetrical stenciling is a more elaborate and unusual example of a decorative arts border. Original colors and stencils were used to replace the sun room's design. The artists painted new patterns for the upstairs bedrooms with the help of reference books and their own creative inspiration.

Hampton Roy and Becky Witsell found the buckeye pattern now decorating a guest bedroom in a 1915 stencil book. "We thought it would look nice and it fits the space," Hampton explains. "It was really interesting to work with an artist and see how they develop a rhyme or reason in what they do. The bathroom off that bedroom has a diamond-shaped pattern in the stained-glass window, so Becky matched the room's stenciling detail to that design."

Other elements of the house were gradually pieced together like a giant jigsaw puzzle. Before the Roys first saw the house, a real estate agent, when visiting the property one afternoon, found unassembled bannisters and balustrades stacked in the entry ready for removal by vandals. She stored them in her own home until the Roys' restoration work began. The Roys were not as lucky when seeking to replace the floor-to-ceiling entry hall mirror. Though the Roys were able to track the original mirror down in Memphis, Tennessee, the family who bought it from an architectural salvage company was unwilling to sell it to them. So, instead, a reproduction now hangs in the Cornish house.

The Roys did successfully locate lead glass panes that had been removed from the house. After they moved in, a salvage artist sold the original front door panes back to them for $300. An upstairs bedroom and bath's five windows turned up when a Quapaw Quarter policeman returned the originals he had taken home for safekeeping.

Restoration specialists advised the Roys that all of the relocated panes were from the 1934 renovation instead of the 1916 construction. Fiercely determined to return the house to its

original glory as much as possible, the Roys followed the 1916 plans and had the patterns of the existing windows duplicated in smaller-sized panes. The owners bought the windows for the library from Little Rock's St. Andrews Catholic Cathedral; the cathedral windows had been removed and stored for several years in the church basement with other architectural effects.

Roy's description of Ed Cornish as a "forward-thinking guy" indicates how much the preservationist grew to admire his home's builder during the restoration process. The strength of Cornish's vision still lingers in the practical yet elegant imprint he left on the house. "I always think every room has a gender," explains Nancy. "But I think of the whole house as fairly masculine. It is not prissy like a Victorian. It is real solid. We actually live all over the house because you don't have to feel you need to be careful about breaking anything."

The Roys use the house to entertain on a grand scale. They frequently open it up for fund-raising occasions and charity

tours. The first of such functions was a 1981 tour that opened the house up to four thousand visitors, including original resident Hilda Cornish, Ed's daughter. Hilda was fifteen when her family moved into their grand residence and her firsthand accounts personalized the house's history. "She could tell me where she had sparked with different guys throughout the house," says Hampton. "We found on a back stair a heart shape with her initials and a young man's carved in the wood. And it was not the fellow she married."

The house now stands as a footnote in Little Rock's architectural history. Hampton passionately accepted the challenge of saving the landmark home by collaborating with craftsmen and artists. Summarizing the result of all their achievements, Hampton says, "People are desperately trying to save houses and renovate them in downtown neighborhoods everywhere. This house is one of those restoration efforts that has been particularly good."

■■■■■■■■■■■■■■■■
A stenciled border repeats the diamond pattern of a guest bath's single lead-glass window (far left).

■■■■■■■■■■■■■■■■
A full-length mirror reflects the images of the Austrian brass and wood twin beds in an upstairs bedroom (near left).

■■■■■■■■■■■■■■■■
A collection of art glass goblets and decanter adorn a guest room dresser (right).

■■■■■■■■■■■■■■■■
A mirror hanging over a marble-topped chest catches the reflection of an upstairs bedroom furnished with Austrian brass and wood twin beds (above).

SOURCES

■■■■■■■■■■■■■■■■■■■

ANTIQUES & ACCESSORIES

AMERICAN STERLING GALLERIES
195 King Street
Charleston, South Carolina
29401
(803) 723-7197
Obsolete and active sterling flatware patterns and holloware at discounted prices.

ANTIQUIX
275 Peters Street S.W.
Atlanta, Georgia 30316
(404) 688-2010
Craftsman Scott Mullen restores vintage trunks of all styles and sizes.

ARTHUR SMITH
1 West Jones Street
Savannah, Georgia 31401
(919) 236-9701
Houses four floors of eighteenth- and nineteenth-century furnishings.

BIRLANT & CO.
191 King Street
Charleston, South Carolina
29401
(803) 722-3842
Importers of eighteenth- and nineteenth-century English antiques.

CANNON MALL
3509 Broad Street
Chamblee, Georgia 30341
(404) 458-1662
Collection of eight dealers specializing in southern, country-style antiques.

CHARLES COOPER
834 Chartres Street
New Orleans, Louisiana
70130
(504) 523-4718
Beautiful selection of museum-quality Baroque and Renaissance furniture.

CHERRY TREE ANTIQUES
111 East Main Street
Jonesboro, Tennessee 37659
(615) 753-2888
Country antiques and accessories.

COLES & CO.
85 Wentworth Street
Charleston, South Carolina
29401
(803) 723-2142
Direct importers of eighteenth- and nineteenth-century English antiques.

COUNTRY JUNCTION ANTIQUES
314 Rock Knoll Drive
Greenwood, South Carolina
29646
(803) 229-1529
Top-quality early American primitive antiques.

EIGHT FLAGS ANTIQUE MARKET
604 Centre Street
Fernandina Beach, Florida
32034
(904) 277-8550
Diverse collection of antiques and accessories ranging from Adirondak chairs to heirloom wicker tables, quilts, and vintage kitchen accessories.

J.E. GUERCIO ANTIQUES
701 Franklin Street
Natchez, Mississippi 39120
(601) 442-5941
Specializes in nineteenth-century Americana antiques and objects of merit.

HARRISON HOUSE ANTIQUES
1433 Harrison Street
Vicksburg, Mississippi
39180
(601) 638-2178
An eclectic mixture of heirloom collectibles and delicious tea room combination.

HASTENING ANTIQUES, LTD.
1 West Washington Street
Middleburg, Virginia 22117
(703) 687-5664
And
2300 Peachtree Road
Atlanta, Georgia 30309
(404) 351-5489
Both locations carry seventeenth- and eighteenth-century French and English antiques.

HERRON HOUSE
422 Herron Street
Montgomery, Alabama
(205) 265-2063
Large stock of eighteenth- and nineteenth-century furnishings, porcelain, glass, and silver.

JON ANTIQUES
4605 Magazine Street
New Orleans, Louisiana
70130
(504) 899-4482
Inventory of fine English and French eighteenth- and nineteenth-century furnishings as well as period accessories.

JON ERIC RIIS
875 Piedmont Avenue
Atlanta, Georgia 30309
(404) 881-9847
Specialist in antique Oriental textiles and costumes. By appointment only.

LIVINGSTON ANTIQUES
163 King Street
Charleston, South Carolina
29401
(803) 723-9697
Showroom for a 30,000-square-foot warehouse filled with fine antiques.

LOW COUNTRY WALK
Longview Center
1627 Frederica Road
St. Simons Island, Georgia
31522
(912) 638-1216
Diverse mix of European antique furnishings, collectibles, and textiles.

MARTHA SMITH
217 North Main Street
Greenville, South Carolina
29601
(803) 232-6313
Booth specializing in early American antiques. Found inside the Downtown Antiques Mall.

MELOSI, INC.
2300 Peachtree Road
Atlanta, Georgia 30309
(404) 352-5451
Italian and Scandanavian antique furnishings, contemporary European fabrics, and accessories.

PARVIZIAN
612 Bienville Street
New Orleans, Louisiana
70130
(504) 522-1200
Importer of fine hand-woven Persian, Romanian, Chinese, and Pakistani rugs. Nationwide shipping available.

THE PLANTATION SHOP
4806 First Coast Highway
Amelia Island, Florida
32034
(904) 261-2030
Fine European furnishings and antique sterling and porcelain collectibles.

REEDY RIVER ANTIQUES
220 Howe Street
Greenville, South Carolina
29607
(803) 242-0310
American country antiques and accessories.

RIVER CITY ANTIQUES
1500 Washington Street
Vicksburg, Mississippi
39180
(601) 638-4758
American and European antiques. Same company holds frequent auctions of estate items.

ROGER THOMAS, LTD.
#1210B, 8401 9th Street
St. Petersburg, Florida
33702
Antique horse and dog porcelain figurines, oil paintings, and prints.

SIMONTON ANTIQUES
620 Franklin Street
Natchez, Mississippi 39120
(601) 442-5216
American antiques from the eighteenth- and nineteenth-century.

THE TABBY HOUSE
105 Retreat
St. Simons Island, Georgia
31522
(912) 638-2257
English antiques and Low-Country furnishings.

TURNER ANTIQUES
GALLERY
815 North Baylen Street
Pensacola, Florida 32501
(904) 432-6434
English antiques and heirloom paintings and decorative accessories.

VENDUE HOUSE
ANTIQUES
9 Queen Street
Charleston, South Carolina
29401
(803) 577-5462
*Fine eighteenth- and
nineteenth-century English
antiques and art.*

VILLAGE GREEN
ANTIQUE MALL
424 North Main Street
Hendersonville,
North Carolina 28792
(704) 692-9057
*Large variety of antiques and
accessories—from cups to
cupboards—of all periods and
styles sold by over fifty dealers.*

WIRTHMORE ANTIQUES
5723 Magazine Street
New Orleans, Louisiana
70130
(504) 897-9727
*French Provincial furnishings
from the eighteenth- and
nineteenth-century: fruitwood
buffets, armoires, farm tables,
and more. Custom-made
lamps also available.*

ART & CRAFT GALLERIES

ATTIC GALLERY
1406 Washington Street
Vicksburg, Mississippi
39180
(601) 638-3987
*Paintings, pottery, handmade
baskets, and local crafts by
local artists.*

BERMAN GALLERY
1131 Euclid Avenue
Atlanta, Georgia 30307
(404) 525-2529
*Represents Georgia native
Howard Finster and other folk
artists. Also, sculpture and
contemporary ceramics from
local craftspeople.*

CHIHAUHAU GALLERY
400 Julia Street
New Orleans, Louisiana
70130
(504) 523-7411
*Fibers, jewelry, glass, wood,
and ceramics by craftspeople
throughout the nation with a
special emphasis on regional
works.*

CONNELL GALLERY/
GREAT AMERICAN
GALLERY
333 Buckhead Avenue
Atlanta, Georgia 30305
(404) 261-1712
*Specializes in museum-quality
American art and craft media
such as clay, glass, metal,
wood, and fiber.*

ENDANGERED SPECIES
619 Royal Street
New Orleans, Louisiana
70130
(504) 568-9855
*Extensive collection of primitive
art, tribal jewelry, and antique
ivory.*

THE FOLK CENTER
P.O. Box 9545
Asheville, North Carolina
28815
*Resource for homespun
Appalachian textiles, pottery,
crafts, and other original
artworks. Located on the Blue
Ridge Parkway at milepost 382.*

GALLERIE SIMONNE
STERN
518 Julia Street
New Orleans, Louisiana
70130
(504) 529-1118
*Represents regional, national,
and international artists.*

GALLERY WEST INDIES
102 Church Street
Charleston, South Carolina
29401
(803) 720-8876
*Represents area artists as well
as works by North American
artists, pre-Columbian art,
and museum-quality West
Indian art.*

GASPERI GALLERY
320 Julia Street
New Orleans, Louisiana
70130
(504) 524-9373
*Specializes in regional
outsider/folk art.*

GRANNY'S GALLERY
109 East Main Street
Jonesborough, Tennessee
37659
(615) 753-9567
*Represents owner/artist
Barbara Ferrell who paints
primitive landscape scenics.*

LOWCOUNTRY
ARTISTS, LTD.
87 Hasell Street
Charleston, South Carolina
29401
(803) 577-9295
*Paintings, woodcuts, pottery,
and prints by nine Charleston
artists.*

MAIN STREET GALLERY
641 Main Street
Clayton, Georgia 30525
(404) 782-2440
*Crafts, visionary folk art, and
funky, handmade furniture.*

THE OAKS GALLERY
U.S. Highway 441
Dillsboro, North Carolina
28725
(704) 586-6542
*A complex featuring tradi-
tional and contemporary
crafts from more than sixty
Appalachian artisans.*

OUT OF THE WOODS
22-B Bennett Street
Atlanta, Georgia 30309
(404) 351-0446
*Fine art and crafts gallery
specializing in wood and
Native American art.*

PIEDMONT CRAFTSMEN'S
SHOP AND GALLERY
411 North Cherry Street
Winston-Salem,
North Carolina 27101
(919) 725-8243
A showcase for southern crafts.

SEVEN SISTERS GALLERY
49 Broadway Street
Asheville, North Carolina
28815
(704) 669-5107
*Mix of traditional and con-
temporary, functional, and
decorative crafts.*

SIGNATURE SHOP
3267 Roswell Road
Atlanta, Georgia 30305
(404) 237-4426
*The oldest in the city with a
selection that ranges from ceramic mugs to museum-quality,
hand-turned wooden bowls.*

TOUCHSTONE GALLERY
508 North Main Street
Hendersonville,
North Carolina 28792
(704) 692-2191
*Emphasis on contemporary
American paintings, sculpture, and glass by leading
regional artists.*

URBAN NIRVANA
15 Waddell Street
Atlanta, Georgia 30307
(404) 688-3329
*Functional art for the home
and garden by gallery owner
Christine Sibley, plus rotat-
ing shows by local craftspeople.*

VIRGINIA FOUCHE
BOLTON ART GALLERY
127 Meeting Street
Charleston, South Carolina
29401
(803) 577-9351
*Original paintings and
limited-edition lithographs
of Charleston scenes.*

FURNITURE

AXIS TWENTY, INC.
200 Peachtree Hills Avenue
Atlanta, Georgia 30305
(404) 261-4022
*Contemporary twentieth-
century furniture and art
including designs by Eliel
and Eero Saarinen, Patrick
Naggar, Phillipe Starck,
Joe Duke, and others.*

CURREY & COMPANY
45 Bennett Street
Atlanta, Georgia 30309
(404) 351-5115
*A comprehensive resource of
American antiques and handcrafted furnishings for indoors
and outdoors, with an emphasis on southern folk art and
collectibles.*

EMBELLISHMENTS
132 East Bay Street
Charleston, South Carolina
29401
(803) 577-7678
*Garden furniture, stained
glass, weather vanes, and
more.*

237

GARY MIMMS
P.O. Box 3403
Nashville, Tennessee 37219
(615) 297-3155
This Nashville craftsman produces a distinctive line of new American furniture and accessories, including a regionally-flavored collection of little log birdhouses. Printed brochure of the collection is available.

HANNON & SON
37 Cedartown Road
Cave Spring, Georgia 30124
(404) 777-8342
Handcrafted country-style furniture based on eighteenth- and nineteenth-century designs.

HISTORIC CHARLESTON
REPRODUCTIONS
105 Broad Street
Charleston, South Carolina
29401
(803) 723-8292
Complete resource for furniture, decorative objects, fabrics, wallpaper, and porcelain by American and European companies authorized by the Historic Charleston Foundation Royalties.

LEDFORD
60 Oakgrove Road
Franklin, North Carolina
28734
(704) 524-6744
Woodworker Phil Ledford custom crafts fine furnishings and cabinets.

LEITMOTIF
434 Julia Street
New Orleans, Louisiana
70130
(504) 525-5050
Contemporary lighting, furniture, and objects by modern masters: Aalto, Mies, Corbusier, and others.

MARIO VILLA GALLERY
3908 Magazine Street
New Orleans, Louisiana
70130
(504) 895-8731
Shop features the metal, neo-classic furniture designs of artist/owner Mario Villa.

RATTANWORKS
349 Peachtree Hills Avenue
Atlanta, Georgia 30305
(404) 237-6765
Design source for contemporary classic furnishings and quality reproductions.

THOMAS ELFE
WORKSHOP
54 Queen Street
Charleston, South Carolina
29401
(803) 722-2130
Excellent eighteenth-century reproductions such as Charleston rice beds, handmade mirrors, as well as silverplate, pewter, and porcelain.

FINISHING TOUCHES

FREDERICKSBURG
PEWTER
26 Cumberland Street
Charleston, South Carolina
29401
(803) 577-0626
Plates, mugs, bowls, and original designs made on commission.

GOODWIN WEAVERS
West Cornish Road
Blowing Rock,
North Carolina 28605
(704) 295-3577
Sells bedspreads, tablecloths, and afghans created on Civil War-era looms.

IVAN BAILEY
METAL STUDIO
887 West Marietta Street,
N.W.
Atlanta, Georgia 30318
(404) 874-7674
Master designer/craftsman of metal and iron who specializes in architectural iron and other metal work for the home—gates, railings, chandeliers, table's bases, and more.

NORTHSIDE
RESTORATIONS, INC.
500 Bishop Street
Atlanta, Georgia 30318
(404) 355-5793
Specializes in antique furnishing repairs and refinishing.

SKEMA
587 Dutch Valley
P.O. Box 8598
Atlanta, Georgia 30306
(404) 892-8400
A trio of female artists whose custom-designed patterns for home furnishing surfaces detail everything from rugs to curtains.

238

WOODEN-MYER
1419 Woodmont Lane
Atlanta, Georgia 30318
(404) 350-9730
*Specialists in custom cabinets
and trellises.*

WORTHINGTON
GROUP, LTD.
652 Miami Circle
Atlanta, Georgia 30324
(404) 872-1608
*Specializes in replacement ar-
chitectural design elements
such as posts and columns.*

PLANTS

BAYCREEK GARDENS
P.O. Box 339
Grayson, Georgia 30221
(404) 339-1600 or
(800) 548-8227
*Leading mail-order supplier
of rhododendrons, mountain
laurel, azaleas, and leucothoe.
Free catalogs available. Door-
step delivery.*

GOODNESS GROWS
156 South Woodlawn Drive
Crawford, Georgia 30630
(404) 743-5055
*Emphasis on unusual peren-
nials and herbs.*

JOHN HOWARD &
ASSOCIATES
1293 Peachtree Street
Suite 701
Atlanta, Georgia 30309
(404) 876-7051
*Landscape architecture firm
specializing in custom-
designed residential gardens.*

LOST MOUNTAIN
NURSERY
824 Poplar Spring Road
Lost Mountain, Georgia
30132
(404) 427-5583
*Specialize in perennials,
herbs, and unusual plant
varieties for indoor and
outdoor use.*

LYNCHBURG FLORIST
AND ANTIQUES
3224 Old Forest Road
Lynchburg, Virginia 24503
(804) 385-6566
*Danny Snapp creates casual
and formal floral designs.*

WINDMILL GARDENS
P.O. Box 351
Luverne, Alabama 36049
(205) 335-5568
*A source for unusual and
unique daylilies.*

ARCHITECTS AND DESIGNERS

SUZANNE ALLEN
Suzanne B. Allen &
Company Design
176 Peachtree Hills Avenue
Atlanta, Georgia 30305
(404) 231-4424

THOMAS A. BLOUNT
484 Randall Mill Road,
N.W.
Atlanta, Georgia 30327
(404) 233-9444

BUZZ HARPER
Simonton Antiques
620 Franklin Street
Natchez, Mississippi 39120
(601) 442-5216

STEVEN HARRIS
285 Broadway
New York, New York 10007
(212) 587-1108

JACK MITCHELL
Mitchell, Small & Donehue
Architects
10 North Atlantic Wharf
Charleston, South Carolina
29401
(803) 723-3407

SKIP TUMINELLO
S.J. Tuminello, Architect
and Associates
1010 Monroe Street
Vicksburg, Mississippi
39180
(601) 636-0033

JIM WESTERFIELD
Westerfield Antiques
and Interiors
4429 Old Canton Road
Jackson, Mississippi 39211
(601) 362-7508

BIBLIOGRAPHY

■■■■■■■■■■■■■■■■■■■■■■■■■■■■■

BOOKS

Bartley, Numan. *The Evolution of Southern Culture*. Athens, GA: The University of Georgia Press, 1988.

Billington, Monroe Lee. *The American South*. New York, NY: Charles Scribner's Sons, 1971.

Boney, Nash. *Southerners All*. Macon, GA: Mercer University Press, 1984.

Cangelosi, Robert, and others. *New Orleans Architecture*. Gretna, LA: Pelican Publishing Company, Inc., 1989.

Cate, Margaret. *Early Days of Coastal Georgia*. New York, NY: The Gallery Press, 1955.

Coleman, Kenneth. *Colonial Georgia*. New York, NY: Charles Scribner's Sons, 1976.

Ferris, William, and Reagan, Charles. *Encyclopedia of Southern Culture*. Chapel Hill, N.C.: University of North Carolina Press, 1989.

Hesseltine, William, and Smiley, David. *The South in American History*. Englewood Cliffs, NJ: Prentice-Hall, Inc., 1960.

Lane, Mills. *Architecture of the Old South—Georgia*. Savannah, GA: Beehive Press, 1986.

Lane, Mills. *Architecture of the Old South—Mississippi/Alabama*. Savannah, GA: Beehive Press, 1989.

Lane Mills, *Architecture of the Old South—South Carolina*. Savannah, GA: Beehive Press, 1984.

Lane, Mills. *Architecture of the Old South—Virginia*. Savannah, GA: Beehive Press, 1987.

Leckie, George. *Georgia—A Guide to its Towns*. Atlanta, GA: Tupper & Love, 1940.

Lester, Jim, and Lester, Judy. *Greater Little Rock*. Norfolk, VA: The Donning Company Publishers, 1986.

Little, John. *Butler County Alabama 1815 to 1885*. Cincinnati, OH: Elm Street Printing Company, 1885.

McAlester, Lee, and McAlester, Virginia. *A Field Guide to American Houses*. New York, NY: Alfred A. Knopf, 1990.

McGill, Ralph. *The South And The Southerner*. Boston, MA: Little, Brown & Company, Ltd., 1959.

Morgareidge, Kay. *Foundations of Government—The Georgia Counties*. Atlanta, GA: Hill R. Healan, 1976.

Roller, David, and Twyman, Robert. *The Encyclopedia of Southern History*. Baton Rouge, LA: Louisiana State Press, 1979.

Roy, Hampton. *Charles L. Thompson and Associate Arkansas Architects 1885–1938*. Little Rock, AK: August House, 1982.

Roy, Hampton, and Witsell, Charles. *How We Lived: Little Rock As An American City*. Little Rock, AK: August House, 1984.

Wilson, Everett. *Early Southern Towns*. London, GB: A.S. Barnes & Company, Inc., 1967.

Wood, Wayne. *Jacksonville's Architectural Heritage*. Jacksonville, FL: University of North Florida Press, 1989.

PERIODICALS

Bahr, Bob. "Positively 14th Street." *Atlanta*, November 1986, pp. 56–59.

Boineau, John. "Early Colonial Settlers of Summit Plantation on the Toogoodoo." *Hugenot Society of South Carolina*, 1981, pp. 80–83.

Freiman, Ziva. "A Rebel in the Suburbs." *Metropolitan Home*, April 1989, pp. 152–156.

Hanle, Zack. "A Super Southern Picnic." *Bon Appétit*, August 1986, pp. 60–95.

Landis, Dylan. "Collector's Addition." *Metropolitan Home*, October 1990, pp. 150–155.

Langley, Lynne. "Summitt House." *The News & Courier*, July 7, 1985, pp. 1–3.

Mashburn, Rick. "Collective Genius." *Historic Preservation News*, July, 1990, pp. 50–55.

Mays, Vernon. "Local Color." *Progressive Architect*, December 1988, pp. 82–87.

Ross, Margaret. "The Building of the Quapaw Quarter." *Quapaw Quarter: Guide to Little Rock's 19th-century Neighborhoods*, 1976.

Sewell, Cliff. "Beaulieu." *Savannah News-Press*, April, 1974.

Sweeney, Thomas. "Charleston On the Mend." *Historic Preservation News*, October 1990, pp. 24–81.

Wilkinson, Constance. "Hugenots on Laurel Hill." *Hugenot Society of South Carolina*, 1979, pp. 83–99.

Wilson, Susannah. "Cliff-hanger Rescue." *Southern Accents*, April 1990, pp. 96–103.

Wojtas, Edward. "Waltzing through the tip of northeastern Tennessee." *The Atlanta Journal–The Atlanta Constitution*, July 29, 1990, p. 1.